Teaching the Art of Filmmaking

KAREN BENNETT

Copyright © 2017 Karen Bennett
All rights reserved.
ISBN-13: 978-1974229925

DEDICATION

This book is dedicated to Karen and Jim Covell, Alison Farr, Deana Payne, and Genevieve Colvin for their incredible support and encouragement.

CONTENTS

		Preface	i
Part I		Building a Positive Classroom Environment	1
	1	Controlling the Class Discussions	3
	2	Always Be Learning	6
	3	Make it Okay to Fail	7
	4	Give the Weird Idea a Shot	8
	5	Give them Boundaries	11
	6	Set Clear Expectations	18
Part II		Teaching the Art of Filmmaking	27
	1	What's Your Curriculum?	28
	2	Blocking Out the Year	31
	3	Teaching Screenwriting	33
	4	Handling Auditions	49
	5	Assembling Your Film Crews	52
	6	Pre-Production Crew Meetings	59
	7	Production	61
	8	Editing	65
	9	Copyright Concerns	73
	10	Every Day Warm Ups	75
Part III		Behind the Scenes	83
		Followed	84
		Thriller	89
		Slenderman	95
		Confronting #8	101
		The Redemption of Allen Lineman	107
		Millikan Votes 2016	116
		Final Thoughts	123

PREFACE

I began my teaching career after four years of freelance music editing in the film and television industry. While working on *Cats and Dogs* I took the CBEST test. While working on *Harry Potter and the Prisoner of Azkaban* I took my credentialing classes. I intended to leave Los Angeles. The stress of being freelance was not something I could see managing in the long term. If I was working, that was great! I could afford to live comfortably, but the question was: what if I don't get another job right away? I had always loved working with kids, I loved English and History; so the answer seemed obvious: teach! Teachers have a set schedule, a predictable (if small) paycheck, and who wouldn't love working with kids all day? I could even move away from expensive and crazy Los Angeles. I could work in a small but beautiful mountain town somewhere far from the 405 Freeway! What a fabulous way to make a meaningful impact on the world! (I'm choking back a laugh as I'm writing this.)

Due to an influx of teachers the year I finished my credential, there were no teaching positions available for English or History teachers in any beautiful mountain towns. Nobody wanted to hire me. It was just too competitive. Finally out of a last ditch "what the hell" moment, I gave in and submitted my resume to Millikan Middle School and Performing Arts Magnet in my own neighborhood not far from the 405 Freeway. Since it was a performing arts school, I tweaked my resume to include some of my film work and was immediately hired. I was going to be staying in Los Angeles.

Teaching is by far the hardest job I have ever had. People will blow off that sentence when they read it, so I'll say it again: Teaching is by far the hardest job I have ever had. This includes working as a music editor for James Cameron as he tried to save his TV show *Dark Angel* from cancellation. Yep. Teaching is harder than working for James Cameron.

To my reader, I love that you are trying to navigate inside the world of education to bring the art of filmmaking to the youngest generation. You already have my sincerest good wishes. I hope this book will give you some answers. I hope in reading about my missteps you'll avoid doing the same. I hope at the end of each day you are reminded that we are in this together.

Part I: Building a Positive Classroom Environment

The Most Important Information in This Book has Nothing to Do With Filmmaking

It does not matter how much money you fundraise for equipment, how much support you have from your administrators, how brilliant your students are, or how much experience you have in filmmaking *if you do not foster a sense of compassion, collaboration, and respect in your classroom.*

This can be said for teaching any subject, any grade, and it is the reason teaching is such a difficult job to do well. Students need to feel safe enough in your classroom to fail or they will never reach beyond their comfort zone. Parents need to believe that you truly *like* their kids or you'll never be able to address the difficulties that come with learning as a team. Mutual respect is key.

If you truly do not *like* children, then back away slowly and find another career. If you can't find humor in eye rolling and excuses for late assignments, then this isn't for you. Teaching will try your patience every day. Students at all levels of education are there because *they are learning*, so if you cannot deal with seeing the same mistakes year after year as new groups of young people pass through the doors of your classroom then you are in the wrong profession.

I have not yet met a parent who isn't skeptical when they walk into my classroom for the first time. They are skeptical because they don't know if they want to trust me with their child's education and I don't blame them! It is my job to earn their trust through creating a positive environment for their child. Do I screw it up sometimes? Yep! The good news is that parents will stand by you when they see that you honestly like their child and you believe their child can do well.

Building a Positive Classroom Environment:
1: Controlling the Class Discussions

Would you pour your heart, time, energy, and passion into a school project if you believed your peers were going to be critical of it and judge you for it? Nah. I wouldn't either. In our society today we have this odd perspective that making a negative or critical comment makes us sound more intelligent than a positive or respectful one. Listen to people as they walk out of a movie theater and you will inevitably hear, "What a stupid ending," or "Ugh, I just can't stand that actor." Go ahead and check out the comments section on YouTube (but not for long or you might fear for the future of our civilization). I can guarantee the students in your classroom will tend towards negative comments when viewing a short film. To be critical in a negative way somehow equates to intelligence and that is something that must change in order to foster a positive environment in your film class.

I love the old proverb: *"A fish rots from the head."* How are YOU handling criticism? My kids on a Monday will come up to me and ask if I've seen whatever movie opened that weekend. I could say, "I saw the new Michael Bay movie. It had a totally unbelievable plot and if I see one more unnecessary explosion I'm going to scream." OR I could say, "I was really impressed by the practical visual effects in the last action scene. Those stunt actors were really insane to watch! I think stunt choreography should have its own category at the Oscars, what do you think?"

In my classroom I control the conversations. I have a policy that negative comments are never allowed when discussing creative work. When we discuss a child's homework project the class is given the following directives: 1. No talking during the film. 2. Each student in the class must come up with at least two specific aspects of the film that *worked well*.

- "I liked the way the protagonist was introduced in the film."
- "I liked the canted angle that was used when the protagonist realized they had been tricked."
- "I liked the way the music made me really sad when the antagonist realized they needed to apologize."
- "I liked the performance of the lead actress, especially when she had to say goodbye to her best friend before she moved."

The class conversation then progresses exactly this way:

1. When the film ends, I start the conversation with something specific I appreciated about the film.
2. Next, I choose a student to restate my compliment and add a compliment of his or her own. *(I don't allow for hands to be raised so that every child knows they may be called on and might have to respond. This forces them all to listen carefully to everyone's comments.)*
3. I then choose another student at random who has to recap what the previous student said and then add a compliment of his or her own.
4. I will close out the discussion by giving the filmmaker ONE thing to work on for the next project.

Why only one? We all know in a middle school film project there are going to be hundreds of things that need improvement. On any given project the student probably had trouble with: capturing clean sound, lighting, bad performances from their actors, framing, editing for continuity, choppy music editing, titles that are too long/short/misspelled/incomplete etc. So why only one? Because I want the kid to *not* be overwhelmed! If I gave them a laundry list of 72 things that DIDN'T work about a film that they spent WEEKS on, they would very likely give up and feel it wasn't in their power to make a watchable movie. So I give them one aspect to focus on for the next project. Which aspect? Whichever one will make the most difference in their filmmaking for their next film. Why bother telling them their titles are written in a distracting font if their story missed a clear beginning, middle, and satisfying ending? One small step at a time, folks. It's the best way to get them to keep moving forward!

Side Note: As the students watch and give comments about each others' films, they notice what worked about each film and will consider whether or not that aspect was present in their own film. If you have one kid who has really beautiful main titles, then the kids will all veer in that direction on the next project. If one kid creates a beautifully edited montage, the kids will notice and try that technique next time. It kind of goes with the philosophy on correcting someone's pronunciation or grammar: don't. Just use the grammatical phrase or pronounce the word correctly when you are conversing with them in the future and they'll pick up on it without feeling humiliated by a direct correction. This goes for teaching filmmaking too.

Oh! The students in my class will never get the opportunity to say anything negative when we view the students' films. Ever. Why, you ask? Because #1 the filmmaker is already hyper aware of what *didn't* work and #2 when working on their next film projects all of the students will hesitate, anticipating the negative and perceived smug response from their peers. What's the point? No point. No negative comments. They are not helpful. Move on.

Building a Positive Classroom Environment
2: Always Be Learning

A good teacher knows that they don't know everything. This is a tough pill to swallow because it feels like it is our job to know every aspect of the subject we are teaching. In filmmaking the technology and trends are always changing so give up on the idea that you will somehow have all of the answers to every question and know every piece of technology on the market. That is pure insanity. It is okay to say to your class, "I'm not sure, let's look it up on the Internet," "Maybe Andrew Kramer has done a tutorial on that one," or "Let's brainstorm ways we can troubleshoot that problem." Be prepared to continue learning for the rest of your career!

When I began teaching, a master teacher gave me what I think is a brilliant bit of practical advice. She said, "Whatever project you give to the kids, do it first yourself so you can see where it might be hard or need more explanation in your instructions." GREAT! This is helpful when you are giving your English class an essay or a poster project. It can be restrictive, however, when you are asking your students to be artistic.

Here's the Balance: If you're asking the kids to make a movie, you should know a lot about the basic tools you're asking them to use: screenwriting techniques, camera and production equipment, and editing software. If a child comes to you and says, "I have been using some new 3D software that I want to try out on this project," and you have never used that specific 3D software, find a way to have them work that aspect into their project *while at the same time* finding a back door to let them bail on that software if it doesn't work out so they can still finish the project. This is the nearly impossible task of being a good teacher: encourage the kid to crawl out on a limb with a project while providing a parachute in case the limb snaps. Remind them of the number one objective: turn in a finished film. That's it. It doesn't have to be brilliant or even successful. The process of attempting to step outside their comfort zone is to be commended and encouraged. It will not always result in a successful film and that's okay! Which leads me to my next point…

Building a Positive Classroom Environment
3: Make It Okay to Fail

Make it very clear from day one that every student will make an unsuccessful movie. (In our class we call this a "face plant.") Remind them that their favorite alumni in the program have all made movies that bombed. Remind them that you yourself have made movies that bombed. The goal is not to allow the students to settle for making sloppy movies that bomb; the goal is to give them hope when they inevitably do and are disappointed. No child I have ever met wants to come into class with a film that is unwatchable. The policy in my room is that everyone must turn in a film on time and all films will be viewed and discussed as a class. Remember! All comments are positive from the class, so a student who brings in a face plant of a film will hear only the aspects of the film that worked. The one "next step" goal I give that student will be very simple: "I want you to use a tripod on your next film." "Next time, make sure you rehearse your actors before you shoot each scene."

Meet the Robinsons (2007) is an adorable little movie about a family of inventors. In one scene the little boy presents his latest invention of a peanut butter and jelly squirter to the family and the machine fails horribly. The boy is crushed until his family, covered in peanut butter and jelly from the explosion, cheers, "You failed!" His mom says, "From failure you learn, from success; not so much." The family members then go around to state the best times they failed before they succeeded. The family motto is "Keep Moving Forward."

This is exactly the tone you must strike with your students. I work with middle schoolers, but it is totally and completely relevant to high schoolers, college students, and adults!

Building a Positive Classroom Environment
4: Give the Weird Idea a Shot

In 2009 my first film student, Cameron Covell, came into my classroom the last week of school and pitched me his summer movie idea. At that point we didn't have a formal class and he was kind of relegated to after school pre-production conversations with me and summer film shoots around town with his parents and friends. He had made two very successful movies each of the previous summers: *Followed* (which will be discussed in detail later) and *Dreamer,* about a boy with a bully problem and a big imagination. Cameron was already a very accomplished filmmaker, actor, screenwriter, tap dancer, and juggler. I had every reason to have faith in him.

"Ms. Bennett, I have decided what my next summer movie project will be!"

I was tired. The kind of tired that only can be understood by a teacher in the last few weeks of the school year.

"Shoot, kiddo. What have you got for me?"

"It's an original musical about a kid who is an outcast at school because he isn't cool and can't do hip hop so he runs away and meets this old guy in a cave who introduces him to tap dancing so the kid goes back to school and introduces all of the hip hop dancers to tap dancing and then becomes cool." Cameron was obviously excited.

I looked at him trying to imagine the story he was pitching. Coming from a background in post production, film scoring, editing, and knowing middle schoolers and all of their quirks I felt even more tired than when he came into my room a few seconds before. Musicals require an obscene amount of pre-production. A screenplay would have to be written. Songs and lyrics would have to be written and recorded. Dance choreography in both hip hop and tap would have to be figured out and rehearsed. We'd have to find locations where we could set up speakers for playback with actors who could sing, dance, and act at a time of year when nobody was reliably available. All of this in the next nine weeks of summer vacation?

"Kiddo, that is the worst idea you've ever had."

Yep, I said that. To my awesome, smart, funny, talented student. His face fell. My heart leapt up in my throat and broke. I have never in my life wanted to take back words so badly.

"Okay, well I think I can do it and I'm going to work on it," he said looking down.

"Why don't we talk about it tomorrow. This project is going to take way more time then you think."

"Okay, Ms. Bennett. See you tomorrow."

I kicked myself all the way home. I wrote Cameron an email CC'ing his mother with an apology for my words. They forgave me because they are awesome and kind. I resolved to help him make his movie.

That summer we made *Outcast*[1]. We worked on the screenplay back and forth via email while Cameron started writing lyrics to the songs he was working out with his dad who is a film composer. They figured out how to record taps for the soundtrack by researching old Fred Astaire movies. Cameron's tap teacher came on board to play the old man who teaches the kids about tap dancing in the movie. We secured the school as a location. Cameron's dad went into his garage and built a dolly out of old roller blade wheels and PVC piping then he built a jib out of metal pipes and 2x4s. Cameron rallied his friends to be actors. He worked out the choreography with his dancers recruiting the help of our dance teacher, Kristine Graham, who was seven months pregnant and couldn't wait to work on the project with us. Cameron's brother Chris pitched in as cameraman and we began to shoot, dragging speakers around with us for playback on set and schlepping more equipment each day than ever before.

There is no pretty way to make a musical that is written, directed, choreographed, performed, and edited by a thirteen-year-old. It was at times a hot mess and at other times pure, exhausting genius. I just about died of fright when Cameron shot his tap dance routine on roller skates *on top* of cement picnic tables in a park (later that year he freaked me out again by tap dancing backwards up a flight of stairs). I truly think that because Cameron didn't quite know what he was getting himself into, it was easier for him to plow ahead with the production. The movie turned out great. It went on to win five awards including *Best of Festival* at the Dance Camera West Festival in their student division.

What is my point? My point is kids have all kinds of weird and strange ideas about stories. Just because I can't quite see their vision, it doesn't mean it

---

[1] *Outcast*: https://vimeo.com/232121010

won't lead to an amazing result. Have a little faith in their creativity. The adult world seems to have squeezed a lot of the goofiness and creativity out of me, so it's good for me to give them creative freedom. Within reason…

Building a Positive Classroom Environment
5: Give them Boundaries

While I definitely want to encourage creative freedom, I also have to be concerned about the content of the films the kids are making. This is a huge hairy deal at the middle school level and will be a different kind of hairy deal at any other level you're working at which is why we have the MPAA.

Here is how I put it to the kids: movies are arguably the loudest and most powerful art form in modern history. There's a reason why filmmakers were used to create propaganda as far back as WWI and there's a reason why politicians spend so much money on campaign ads today. Filmmakers are people who have at their disposal a huge microphone with which to scream their message be it positive, negative, political, social, or whatever. Be very careful when you step up to the mic and speak through your filmmaking. People will always see it as a reflection of YOU.

Side Note: Please consider doing a short unit on propaganda and filmmaking. My personal favorite is the story behind Charlie Chaplin's *The Great Dictator* but you can use almost any example and get the message across.

With that point made, students need clear and simple guidelines. Sadly, this is where it gets troublesome. Once you make it clear to your students they will not be making movies in the style of Quentin Tarantino (yep, some of my 11-year-olds come to class having seen all of his films *sigh*) it becomes important to parse out the specifics of the rules:

Rule #1: No Swearing

Seems straightforward, except that kids DO swear in real life and we're trying to get the kids to tell stories about their real lives, right Ms. Bennett?

"Is it okay to bleep out the swear words?"

"Is it okay to have the actor say a line that you KNOW is going to end in a swearword that then gets cut off by another actor?"

"What specifically are the swearwords we can't say?"

"Are they all of the George Carlin swearwords?"

"What about Hell"?

"Crap?"

"Damn?"

"Pissed off?"

"What about the difference between the line, "Go to hell," and the line, "I feel like hell"?"

Kids are AWESOME at looking for loopholes. It's their way of showing you their brains are working at full speed. Know your boundaries in this area before you start working with the kids.

Last year my student, Theo, wanted to make a movie called *Crap You*[2] about an evil stuffed bird the protagonist finds at a garage sale. When you turn the bird over, a voice box within it says, "Crap you." What a totally bizarre thing for a stuffed bird to say and yet how appealing to the 10-year-old protagonist! The word "crap" is teetering on the border of inappropriate for middle school but I let it slide because it was so strange and not used in a derogatory way towards a character. When the film won several awards at our Phantom Film Festival I found myself having to say "Crap You" into the microphone in our auditorium.

Rule #2: No Non-School Appropriate Behavior

(No drinking, smoking, drugs, kissing, making out, gambling, super inappropriate clothing, or anything else you'd get sent to the Dean's Office for...)

Miles wanted to make a movie to make a statement about the dangers of smoking. His film, *The Last Cigarette*[3], features his father smoking a cigarette while a young child watches with a voice over poem about the dangers of smoking. The poem was beautifully written and since it had an obviously anti-smoking theme, I permitted it. Nobody bothered to protest or be upset by the on-camera smoking. The response would have been very different if a character in the film was smoking a cigarette in passing or being made to look cool or tough because they were smoking.

---

[2] *Crap You* (2015) by Theo Taplitz: https://vimeo.com/143217350

[3] *The Last Cigarette* (2016) by Miles McCrudden: https://vimeo.com/168473743

Addressing the "on screen kiss": In the previously mentioned film *Dreamer* (2008), my film student Cameron had a storyline with a girl who was dating a bully but then came around at the end to fall for the protagonist. There were two kisses he wrote into the script: one in a nightmare scene where she kisses the bully in front of the protagonist and one at the very end of the film where she kisses the protagonist. During the screenwriting phase it kind of made sense given the journey of the protagonist. Cameron's father wasn't sure it was a good idea, but I had seen multiple middle school plays where the kids had to pull off a stage kiss and it seemed like not a big deal. To be certain, I called up one of our musical theatre teachers and asked how to be sensitive about it. He suggested not having them kiss during rehearsals and when it does happen during the first take, keep it at only a simple peck. Make sure it is low key and don't make a big deal out of it. His advice put me at ease and I allowed the scene.

During the table read, the actors made it seem like it was no big deal. These were kids who had done many plays and films before so they were nonchalant about it.

On the day we filmed, the lead actor got really nervous. He seemed jittery and not okay. When I asked, he said he was nervous that people would see the kiss and judge him on "whether or not he had done it right." My heart went out to him. He was absolutely within his right to be nervous as an actor. I should have listened to Cameron's dad. We changed the shot so he covered up the lens with his hand and it was just assumed that he kissed the girl off screen.

I am not going to judge any theatre productions that include "the kiss" but it is simply not something that I feel kids in middle school are emotionally ready to handle in their personal lives much less on camera in front of a cast and crew.

Rule #3: No Weapons and No Violence

Kids usually understand our "no weapons no violence" rule, but there are some who are completely convinced that their movie will never be cool without a guy with a gun. Be firm. They'll get it if you're clear the answer is no.

"Okay, Ms. Bennett, but what about knives?"

"No."

"But what if they're just being used to chop carrots?"

"Sure!"

"A hammer? What if the guy is hammering a nail then he gets mad and throws it at someone?"

"No."

"What if the hammer is being used and it *accidentally* hits someone?"

"Well..."

"What if someone pushes someone else down?"

"Sounds like physical contact violence—"

"What if someone throws a banana peel on the ground to purposely get someone else to trip on the banana peel?"

"On purpose?"

"What if they *carelessly* throw a banana peel on the ground and someone else *accidentally* trips and falls on the ground?"

"What?!?"

"What if someone punches, stabs, or hurts someone but you don't SEE it on camera?"

"So we *hear* the violence?"

"Yeah!"

"No."

Yep, these have all legitimately come up in my "no violence, no weapons" conversations in the classroom.

The keyword for me is INTENT. In my classroom the definition of violence is, "An action with the *intention* of inflicting physical pain on people or animals." This seems to cover all of their "what ifs." (That definition took me about three years to polish so it was short enough for them to remember

14

and still blocked most of their loopholes.)

Big problem: A good story is born of conflict. Let's take the story idea you will inevitably get from one of the kids: a student is being bullied at school. You have to *show* the protagonist being bullied or else your entire story doesn't get a proper setup. You have to introduce the bully to the audience and in order for us to understand the conflict; we have to *see* the bully doing the bullying! Is it a comedy? Okay, then the bullying incident might be something kind of silly like tying kids' shoelaces together while they're eating lunch. Is it a drama? Now it's going to get harder because the administrators and parents are going to *hate* seeing a kid get slammed into a locker on screen.

Work Around: Make sure you consider the message in the film. If you have a film about bullying then your theme should be about standing up for yourself and resolving the conflict in a healthy way. YOU have to control this aspect of the stories you allow the kids to tell. I have had a ton of kids who give me scripts where the protagonist is bullied and it ends when the protagonist beats the antagonist to a bloody pulp and walks away.

"But Ms. Bennett, I want it to feel like *real life*!"

"Really? How often on our campus does a kid get beaten to a bloody pulp?"

"Um…"

"How often on our campus does a kid get punched at all?"

"Um…"

"Never? Okay, then. Pay attention to real life."

It is OUR job to gently pull their story in an appropriate direction. (Bonus for you: You are going to become a crack script doctor because you will be doing this for hundreds of screenplays every semester!)

Rule #4: No Insulting or Stereotyping Genders, Races, Sexual Orientations, Disabilities, Religions, or Cultures:

You should absolutely bring this up with your class. Allow the kids to ask questions. Remind them we want to see all kinds of different people in their films because we live in a world where every day we interact with people who don't look like us or have the same beliefs that we do.

"Ms. Bennett, what about having a character say, 'Jesus, it's hot in here!'?"

"Not a good idea, kiddo."

"But, I'm not Christian so who cares if *I* say, 'Jesus' in my film?"

"People who believe it is disrespectful to make that word into an interjection or the equivalent of a swearword."

"Oh, okay, then I'll just have him say, "Dang, it's hot in here."

"Yep, there you go."

All of this will come up, I promise you. Don't shy away from a simple and calm explanation then move on.

The Bottom Line: Don't let your students go into production on a film that is not appropriate. It is a huge let down when they've done a ton of hard work and then the film can't be screened because your administrator objects to the content.

A Note on Equity: The boys in my classes tend to write protagonists that are also boys. The girls in my classes write protagonists that are split evenly between boys and girls. Why? It probably has something to do with the lopsided number of white male protagonists in books and Hollywood films, so my kids are emulating what they see.

Keep an eye out for equity in your classroom. If you're making a film as a class, take a look at it before you do acting auditions: is there any particular reason why the protagonist has to be male or female and of a certain ethnic background? Likely not. Cast a wide net when looking for your actors!

On a side note: A few years back I actually had one of my female students say to me, "I don't know why I even try, you know boys make better movies than we do." It didn't matter that she has a female film teacher who highlights the work of female filmmakers. It didn't matter that this very student had produced some absolutely incredible work that had won accolades at multiple student film festivals around the country. I took a deep breath and tried to remember: *middle school is where we are generally at our least confident in our lives.* We may need to give extra encouragement to those students who feel they are outside the stereotype of what a "Hollywood Director" looks like. It doesn't mean that we don't appreciate the work of the white males in Hollywood; they have come so far and done so much that is beautiful and special. To me it means simply that *we haven't yet seen the best of the art form because we haven't yet given all artists an equal chance to put forward their talent in Hollywood.* This generation of students has the best opportunity to change that.

On a positive note: This past spring I had a few children make short films that touched the social issues of immigration and gender stereotypes. Ella made a beautiful film, *Stereo*[4] in which the gender stereotypes are reversed: boys wore dresses, girls did not; boys were not expected to play sports and excel in academics, but girls were. In her short film a young girl rebels against these stereotypes and has a blowout with her mother who does not want her to wear a dress. I hesitated before showing that film at a school wide assembly anticipating the student body would find the images of the boys in the film wearing dresses to be laughable. I worried that they would give a rude and negative response to the film. I held my breath and played the film. The audience of loud 11-14 year olds calmed down. In the scene with the girl confronting her mother about wanting to wear a dress, the audience applauded in support of the protagonist. My heart leapt at the thought of Ella witnessing her film being accepted by the audience. I loved that the middle schoolers had proven me wrong with their warm response.

---

[4] *Stereo*: https://vimeo.com/219417572

Building a Positive Classroom Environment
6: Set Clear Expectations

Don't be Afraid to Discuss Expectations with the Parents and Students:
As your students get more and more advanced, the parents will try to become more involved in the process. We're all familiar with the way a school science fair project becomes a family science fair project when a parent helps too much. This leads to fights within the family and can have a detrimental affect on the child's love of the subject. Sometimes parents just can't help themselves. They see their child shooting a movie and they just need to give some advice or show them how they think it's supposed to be done. They desperately want to see their child succeed and sometimes even become a bit competitive with other parents over their child's work.

I've had lots of experience with parent participation in our Cinematic Arts Academy. I honestly really love all of the parents; they mean well! But what do you do when parents become problematic? You have to start early with expectations for them at the beginning of the school year. Yes, *before* they become too involved or give negative criticism of their child's work, you have to talk to them about *how to be a parent of a young filmmaker*. They weren't born knowing this stuff! This applies to parents who know absolutely nothing about filmmaking and it applies equally to parents who may have a job in the film industry and think they know *everything* about how their child should go about making a movie.

I come from being a freelance music editor in the film industry, so here is the truth: people who are working in the industry are a small cog in a huge machine. No one in the industry does every part of the filmmaking process by themselves. Steven Spielberg relies on Janusz Kaminski for the beautiful cinematography in his films and Michael Kahn for the editing of his films. I've heard him speak many times about how grateful he is for the amazing crew he gets to work with.

Now, take a step back and look at your 11-year-old student (or your 16-year-old student or your 19-year-old student). They do not have the confidence or resources of Steven Spielberg. For their first few films, they will be doing all parts of the filmmaking process on their own with only the help of their actors and friends. They will be the writer, director, grip, lighting, sound, wardrobe, props, and editorial crew. All of these jobs are new to them and they are making the rookie mistakes that everyone makes *in all these areas* during their first few films. Do you have some extra love for them now? Do you see why we need to be as supportive and non-critical as possible? Going through this process is an absolutely incredible learning experience. The process needs to be fun because the product is not going to be good the first few times out. The parents need to be on board with you on this. I've had many students say they want to give up because, "Mom told me my movie wasn't very good." In this case, Mom missed the entire point of her 11-year-old making a movie.

A few years back I went to my friend, Karen Covell, to brainstorm some Do's and Don'ts for parents of young filmmakers. Her boys, Chris and Cameron, started making films when they were very young. Chris graduated from Chapman University and Cameron graduated from USC Cinematic Arts this year. In working as Cameron's film teacher when he was in middle school I was impressed with the positive way he went about the filmmaking process and the way his parents patiently encouraged him through his mistakes.

I go over Karen's list with my parents at a start of school parent meeting. Over the years I've had many parents tell me this list gives them peace of mind as they watch their kids stumbling through the rookie mistakes in their early films. It's a learning process all the way around…

TOP 10 DOs and DON'Ts FOR PARENTS OF YOUNG FILMMAKERS
by Karen Covell

Dos:
1. If your child wants to make a film, encourage them to do it, even if it's on their cell phone. They are asking to be creative and that will make them a better person.

2. Encourage them to write a good story. That's more important than what equipment they use or how many locations they shoot at. The story is the key and will make a better film. A Red Camera is useless if it's used to shoot a bad story.

3. Make sure you feed your cast and crew on a film shoot. The biggest mistake in shooting a film is not giving all of the cast and crew enough to eat and drink. Food is fuel! Both the kids and their parents will greatly appreciate you feeding the team.

4. Find a healthy balance between parental supervision and a film made by the parents. They need your presence for order, focus, and accountability but they need to make the film themselves. You're there for requested advice and any issues they can't handle, but they need to make the creative decisions and experience both the joys and

the pains of filmmaking on their own.

5. Know that films cost money. The minimum amount needed is for any props, costumes and equipment needed to shoot the story. But you also need a budget for catering meals and having a craft services table set up during the course of production.

6. Encourage your young filmmaker to watch great films. They need to know old films, new films, foreign films, and black & white films. It's best if you watch with them and then lead a discussion afterwards. What was the film saying? What are it's themes and messages? What worked about the storytelling, directing, acting, writing, and editing? The more you discuss films with them the more they will understand the process of making a good film.

7. Be willing to be their Producer. When they finish a script, have a table read with them asking to clarify potential holes in the story or explain the characters. Just saying, "Oh that's good," doesn't help them to become better filmmakers. Help them to understand their budget, go over their scheduling for each day of filming, the night before the shoot go over their equipment making sure batteries are charged, and make sure they have enough time for editing (roughly 3x the length of the shoot). If you have questions, email their teacher.

8. Tell them not to be afraid of making a bad film. Every bad film completed gets them closer to making a good film. It's better to finish making a bad film than never completing a brilliant film. Having a great idea is easy. Actually following through in completing it is brilliant in and of itself.

9. Have fun. Be sure to help shake the stress and keep a healthy perspective. The process should be fun, creative and the environment should promote closer friendships with everyone involved.

10. Have a screening of the film with the cast, crew, and their families. It's a wonderful celebration to have our children make a film and then let everyone involved watch it together regardless of how "good" or "bad" it is. Remember any film that's completed is worth watching. And serve popcorn. Make it a celebration. They have just completed an enormous and creative task!

Don'ts:
1. Don't encourage them to make a film with inappropriate language or sexual content. It's hard enough to make a film, so encourage them to make one that everyone is comfortable about making and watching. They'll have plenty of time to make films that push the envelope later.

2. Don't let them try to do something so big that it will either never happen or will discourage them. At this age they should start small and work up. Often their appetite is bigger than their stomachs and they either get frustrated or don't enjoy the process.

3. Don't tell them their film is bad. Encourage them to finish it. That's the most important goal of the first film. The goal of the next film is to make it one step better than the last one. No film is a failure. It takes a lot of hard work to make a professional looking film and to tell a strong story.

4. Don't make your friends and neighbors mad in the process. Your child needs to learn the limitations of filmmaking as far as what locations work, how much noise you can make, what permission you need to get from neighbors, how early you can start in the morning and how late you can go at night.

5. Don't focus on just the equipment. There is no need to buy them expensive equipment if they can't tell a good story.

6. Don't limit their film education to just watching films. Encourage them to read books, get involved in theatre, go to concerts and write short stories and poetry, doodle, draw graphic novels, whatever it takes to grow in all the arts.

7. Don't lie to them about what their gifts and talents are. If they want to do something in the arts and they really aren't good, then refocus their interest to another art form. They will only get discouraged and frustrated if you encourage them to pursue a gift they don't have.

8. Don't let them give up on a project. Once they start, they need to see it through to the end. The quality is less important than the completed task.

9. Don't let them put filmmaking before their studies. A good filmmaker knows things about many topics and experiences life.

Then they have more to draw upon for their screenplays. A well-balanced person makes a richer storyteller.

10. Don't micromanage their process. Creativity does not fit into a box. The sky's the limit to a storyteller. They need to understand guidelines and the limitations of time and space, but they need the freedom to try new things. Celebrate this process.

What Kind of Outside Help Can They Have? Is it Cheating?

What if a student's next-door neighbor works as a seamstress and can help them make a specific piece of wardrobe for their film? What if their uncle is a carpenter and can help build a specific set piece? What if their mom is a composer and can write music for their film? What if their dad works as a cinematographer and wants to teach them how to use a computerized dolly for one of the shots? What if their grandparents own a horse and they want to use it in their film?

There is a difference between having someone do the work for you and taking advantage of a learning opportunity. If your next-door neighbor is a seamstress, then see if the student can be there to apprentice and help with the designing and assembling of the costume. What a great way to get an appreciation for what the wardrobe department does!

First and foremost the child is a student and therefore any opportunity to learn should be taken advantage of! As a teacher it is our job to make sure the child is always learning. If a child comes to class with a film that has an incredible set piece, have them talk about it to the class! What was it made of? How long did it take? Learning how to hammer and nail something together is every bit as wonderful as learning how to pull off a tilt shot on a tripod!

Last spring, my student, Jack, had a really fantastic idea: he wanted to turn the Shel Silverstein poem *Ickle Me Pickle Me Tickle Me Too*[5] into a short film. His initial concept was to create the inside of the shoe with lots of brown paper bags in a closet at his house. It was a totally brilliant idea and it would have worked well. He was excited about it and got to talking to his uncle who was a set designer. His uncle had a bit of a break in his workload and offered to help Jack design a huge flying shoe out of plaster and chicken wire at his workshop.

---

[5] Ickle Me Pickle Me Tickle Me Too: https://vimeo.com/168689404

In class the next day, Jack raised his hand and said, "Ms. Bennett, I really want to take my uncle up on his offer, but I'm afraid it's cheating because not everyone in the class has access to a workshop like that."

Fortunately the class had wonderful, supportive chemistry and the kids were encouraging of his project. They were able to see that it was a once-in-a-lifetime learning opportunity and everyone was really excited to see what he and his uncle came up with.

Was there some jealousy because he had that opportunity? Probably, but the kids didn't let it get to them. In life we're never on an even playing field. Sometimes we get lucky. I'm not willing to sacrifice a learning opportunity for a kid because it might make another kid jealous.

Nip Gossiping in the Bud

You already know that I do not allow negative criticisms in my classroom, but gossiping is human nature and you will deal with it on multiple levels in your program. A kid who makes a really successful movie will potentially be met with the other kids and parents whispering rumors that, "Her dad did it all for her," or, "Well, you know that boy's aunt is a filmmaker, so…" This has to be shut down firmly. A child who finally has some success with filmmaking will be discouraged if their hard work is met by jealousy and derision by the other kids or their parents.

My policy to the parents: Do not ever speculate on the authenticity of another child's work. That is not for you to judge, but for me as the teacher to assess and deal with. If a parent approaches me to ask about another students' work I simply tell them that my policy is not to discuss a student's work with other parents. I remind them that they would not appreciate it if I discussed their child's work with another parent and that usually gets the point across.

What if the Kid Really Didn't Do the Work Themselves?

So, what if Joe Schmoe *did* turn in a movie that was obviously made by someone else? First of all, let's look at it from Joe's perspective. He's just turned in a movie that is really well made because his aunt who is a professional film editor did the work for him. He knows he cheated.

How Not to Handle It: You may want to ignore your instincts that Joe did not edit the movie himself and play the movie alongside all of the other film projects giving feedback and totally ignoring the impossibly beautiful editing, but that would be a huge disservice to Joe. The next film he makes he now has a bigger problem: either he has to have his aunt edit the movie or he edits it on his own, thereby exposing himself as a cheat when the next film doesn't look nearly as good as the previous one. Joe gets super nervous because he realizes he is going to expose himself as a fraud to the class and to the teacher.

In this scenario, Joe has painted himself into a corner with no way out. Don't let a kid do that.

Better Way to Handle It: Pull Joe aside after class and ask him directly if he edited the film himself. If he lies and says he did, then tell him that this is way above the level of work he is doing in class and you're looking forward to his classwork improving. If he tells the truth and says he didn't, then remind him that his work has to be his own, and he will receive reduced credit on the assignment. Either way, email Joe's parents and have a conference with both the parents and the student.

At the conference, review the filmmaking expectations with Joe and his parents. It is possible (but not likely) that the parents will lie for Joe and tell you he edited the project himself. If they do, give them a simple reminder that you're looking forward to the improvement in his editing skills in the classroom. A family who lies to a teacher is not something you can fix on your own. They have bigger problems than Joe's work in your class. Go home, make yourself a sandwich, and watch some Netflix. Don't let it get you down, because there is only so much you can do. Give Joe an honest grade for the work he does in your class. Eventually it will sort itself out as Joe's aunt no longer wants to make his movies for him or he decides to leave the program because the work is getting harder and he isn't able to keep up.

If during the conference, Joe says he hates editing and has decided he doesn't want to do it, then maybe he needs to pursue another art form. Ask him if he would like a recommendation to get into another elective at the school. Do it in a positive way: not every kid realizes what goes into filmmaking when they join your class! Joe obviously respects you because he turned in the project to begin with and wanted it to look good so he enlisted the help of his aunt. Don't turn your back on him, but instead be the adult who helps him find his way to an art form that he will be passionate about and love!

If during the conference Joe says he lacks confidence in editing, then it is an opportunity to have him come in after school and work on editing with you one-on-one. Editing is complicated and many students just need a few minutes to ask simple questions to get themselves back on track.

If during the conference it comes out that Joe's aunt just got excited that her nephew might be following in her footsteps and overstepped her bounds, then meeting with the parents will probably be a relief when they can tell her that Joe's teacher asked that she not do his work for him.

Did you notice that not once did we ever confront Joe about this in front of the rest of the class? Why? It is NONE OF THEIR BUSINESS! Calling a kid out for cheating in front of the entire class will humiliate them and a humiliated child will not want to work hard for you.

If gossiping gets bad in your class create a policy: "Don't talk about someone in this class unless you're talking to them." I'd rather the kids have conversations about ideas instead of people anyway.

Building a positive classroom environment is tricky and can take a few years to learn to do well. It looks slightly different in every classroom. For me I've found that keeping a sense of humor, reminding myself when I'm busy to pause and really look my students in the eyes and be present when they're talking to me, and encouraging positive feedback at all times will keep me on track to having a successful school year even when difficulties arise.

Part II: Teaching the Art of Filmmaking

Why Teach Filmmaking? Many teachers and parents bemoan our students' love of technology. We shake our proverbial fists at the amount of time kids spend on social media or playing video games citing these as reasons why students have trouble finishing their homework. Teachers can't stand this obsession with technology and yearn after the days when we didn't have smart phones distracting us at the dinner table. For me, the technology age is here and there isn't any use in trying to hold it back. It's changed the way students think and the way they problem solve, so that means that we have to find ways to incorporate technology into the classroom. This absolutely does not mean sticking kids in front of a computer and having them trudge through an online class. The modern world needs creative problem solvers and diplomatic collaborators. We need to find ways to challenge kids using technology in new ways to promote problem solving and teamwork. Filmmaking offers that challenge and kids gravitate toward it because it also offers the opportunity to tell their own stories, relay their nightmares and fears, and try to convince the world of their point of view. When I was little and I'd get bored and pester my dad, he always said, "Buzz off. Go find something constructive to do." Filmmaking is wonderfully constructive.

Chapter 1: What's Your Curriculum?

Sit down and really think about the curricular goals for the program you want to create. This is going to vary depending on your own passion for filmmaking and your background. Don't try to directly replicate what you see others doing because in teaching that almost never works. You will be at your best teaching to your strengths. The following are various ways to approach the goals of filmmaking:

Narrative Storytelling:

When I started my program I knew I wanted to focus on narrative storytelling. My background is in film scoring and I've always been fascinated with telling a story through music so it makes sense that I would continue with narrative work. I wanted to have the kids build to a film festival showcasing their short films at the end of the school year. I wanted them to feel successful and I figured that creating fun short movies that other kids in the school could watch and enjoy would be the best way to go for me.

Super hard challenge in this? Finding the best way to get students to translate their goofy or strange ideas into a school-appropriate story with a clear beginning, middle, and end.

Plus side? Your program will most likely become very popular with the students on campus as they realize how much fun it is to make their unique visions into films.

Double Plus? In the pursuit of writing narrative short films, students tend to get a huge boost in their English comprehension and writing abilities. My students' reading comprehension scores jump up on average 2-3 grade levels during the first year of the program.

Example: Flu Season[6] is a simple narrative written, directed, and edited by our students. They wanted to try some experimental lighting techniques and come up with fun ways to show our protagonist's overactive imagination.

---

[6] *Flu Season:* https://vimeo.com/168778014

Cross-Curricular Filmmaking:

This would entail blending filmmaking with any of the other classes at school. For example: a documentary about the artists of the Renaissance that was researched in history class or a stop motion demonstration of plate tectonics for science class. This typically requires co-planning with the curricular teacher (unless you also teach that curricular class then it becomes easier). If you are a Math, Science, English, or History teacher and want to blend filmmaking into the unit you're working on, this is really fun for the kids. Having the class create an "Epic Rap Battles in History" video is going to be great if the kids have the filmmaking chops required to do this well. Please remember: making a movie is a very long process! Do not assign the project on a Monday to be due the following Friday. In fact, to get the best work from a student in filmmaking be sure to give them at least three weeks to work on a 2-3 minute film because they also have work for other classes to do!

Super hard challenge in this? Trying to make the subject matter come to life in a fun way. Kids will not want to go the extra mile needed to complete a film if the subject matter isn't interesting enough for them. A straight up documentary might not appeal to a 13-year-old as much as a music video for example.

Plus side? The administrators and academic teachers will love you for this. It looks excellent for the school to have students engaged in this type of filmmaking!

Double Plus? Student film festivals often have categories for curricular films that are much less competitive than narrative filmmaking categories. Winning an award at a film festival is a huge incentive for kids to continue making movies the following year!

Example: Odysseus and Polyphemus[7] is a straight retelling of the story from our history unit on Ancient Greece.

Social Activism Filmmaking:

Appeal to your students' sense of social activism and have them create public service announcements to make the world a better place! This might be in

---

[7] *Odysseus and Polyphemus:* https://vimeo.com/230128493

the form of a simple documentary espousing the dangers of peer pressure or it might take the form of a short film, music video, or experimental film with a theme of recycling.

You could also do a weekly news show to share with the rest of the school. This means your production process has to be like clockwork if you're going to crank out one show a week. On this level, having the kids create the logos, intros, outros, music, backgrounds, lower thirds etc. before the first episode even shoots will be key to getting your production flowing.

Super hard challenge in this? It can feel restrictive to the kids when they are brainstorming ideas for news stories or public service announcements. The major social activism themes have been done to death in the world of student filmmaking and the subject matter can be a bit dry and require more patience than kids might have at a young age.

Plus side? Again, your administrators will love seeing your students working on these civic-minded projects. It will make your school look great if the mayor comes to visit!

Example: Us.[8] is a stop motion experimental film by my student Remy that touches on the social issue of immigration in the United States.

Pssst! None of these is any easier than the others. They're all hard to do well.

---

[8] *Us.*: **https://vimeo.com/219408000**

Chapter 2: Blocking Out the Year

Let's say you're interested in making one 5-7 minute narrative movie each semester with your film elective class. Making a movie takes a long time when you can only work on it as a class for 50 minutes a day, five days a week. Keep in mind the inevitable disruptions to the school day (fire drills, assemblies, student absences, etc.) You've got to backward plan to make sure you reach your goal.

Example One Semester Schedule:
At my school each semester is 20 weeks long. If I plan on making a 5-7 minute movie with a class that is brand new to filmmaking in one semester here is my schedule:

2 weeks of basic filmmaking skills: camera angles, film terms, and how to use the equipment.

4 weeks of the basics of screenwriting, brainstorming the concept, and writing the screenplay.

3 days for acting auditions.

1 day for the first table read to iron out any kinks in the script.

1 day to write application letters for crew positions on the shoot.

2 weeks of pre-production including props and wardrobe procurement, scouting and securing locations on campus, and doing test shots for any difficult scenes requiring practical or computer VFX.

During these two weeks, have the kids research short films, commercials, and music videos for wardrobe, music, lighting, and camera angles that inspire them and match the tone they are trying to establish for the film. If appropriate, watch them in class to get a sense of what you're trying to accomplish. It is hard to create one film with so many students and keep the tone consistent. This pre-production work is priceless!

3 days to give the kids their crew positions, scene they are responsible for shooting, and have each crew map out the required props and wardrobe they'll need for their scene. Have the crews also write a shot list for their scenes (I prefer my kids put their shot list in the right hand margin of the script) and a storyboard if necessary.

2 days to do a second table read with our actors. Have the kids take notes regarding blocking and any logistical concerns they have about any of the scenes. This is a good time to figure out a Plan B for any of the really difficult scenes.

4 weeks for Production: Shoot Monday and Wednesday and review footage as a class on Tuesday and Thursday. Prepare for the next week of shooting on Friday. (This assumes I have about eight scenes and am able to shoot one scene a day to minimize problems with continuity within each scene.)

4 weeks for Post Production/Editing: This may vary depending on how complicated the editing task is. If there are lots of visual effects or the students are brand new to editing, make the film shorter and add more days to post production.

The last two weeks are a grace period in case the production schedule got bumped when an actor got sick or the director forgot to push the record button and we need to do reshoots. Something is bound to go wrong, so I give myself some wiggle room here! If everything goes well and we have time left over, I do a mini-unit on specialty titles, credits, color correcting techniques, or work on sound design.

Chapter 3. Teaching Screenwriting

Screenwriting is perhaps the most complex aspect of teaching students to make a movie. Writing a successful story with a beginning, middle, and satisfying end is something that novelists and professional screenwriters struggle with for their entire careers. To ask students at a young age to do this successfully feels like a bit of a stretch. Of course if they don't create a solid story to begin with then no matter how beautiful their work is in production and post-production, the movie will fail.

Proper Screenplay Formatting:

First order of business: Teach the kids proper screenplay formatting through direct instruction. My students are 11 years old when they enter my class. As an English teacher I know kids at this age read novels and see examples of narrative writing all the time; but they still don't have a clue how to properly punctuate dialogue or where to begin and end a paragraph when writing a short story. Teaching them an entirely new writing format is difficult when they're still having trouble with the basic writing conventions. Yep, this is going to take time and patience.

How many of the screenwriting rules do I enforce with my students? Just the basics. In the same way that I don't expect my 11-year-olds to apply every rule in Strunk and White's *Elements of Style* to their writing in my English class, I pick my battles wisely with their screenwriting assignments. They need a simple handout with the basic rules of screenplay formatting they can keep in their binder for reference.

Bonus For You: The kids in my film class jump typically 2-3 grade levels in reading comprehension in one school year. I firmly believe it is because they are being challenged in screenwriting and film analysis. By the end of the year analyzing a novel or short story in English class is child's play for them.

The following is a handout I give my students with the basic elements of screenplay formatting. Students keep this handout in their binder to reference during the school year.

How To Format A Screenplay:

Keep in mind that a screenplay is a roadmap for your cast and crew. Unlike a novel that is intended to be read by a single reader, the screenplay is used by many different people in the cast and crew to know what is required of their job on set. This includes locations needed, blocking, props, wardrobe etc.

Your writing should be visual; your characters' **actions** are the most important part of what we will see in the finished movie. Actions **show** the audience what they need to know. Be sure you are not writing what your character is thinking or writing explanations of backstory if that will not be shown on screen.

Your characters' dialogue should support the actions and the actions should move the story forward.

Movies are made up of **Scenes:** Think of a scene as a unit of action within one location. In each scene, define in your script *who* (characters), *what* (situation), *when* (time of day), *where* (place of action), and *why* (purpose of the action).

Scene Headings: Each time your characters move to a different location, a new scene heading is required *even if a conversation starts in one location and ends in another location!* Why? Because your crew is going to need to know which locations to prep to shoot the conversation!

Scene headings should be typed on one line with some words abbreviated and all words capitalized. The location of a scene is listed before the time of day when the scene takes place.

Example: A scene set outside in the cafeteria during lunch would have the following heading:
EXT. SCHOOL CAFETERIA – LUNCHTIME

Interior means the location is inside a building and is abbreviated INT. Exterior means the location is outdoors and is abbreviated EXT. A dash separates the location of the scene from the time of day. Leave a two-line space following the scene heading before writing your scene description.

Dialogue: Dialogue is centered on the page under the character's name, which is always in all capital letters when used as a dialogue heading.

General: This is where basic information for the scene is given: blocking, props, notes for wardrobe etc. Be sure to capitalize character's names even if the character doesn't have dialogue in the scene.

Action: This is where we give specific movement information in the scene. For example, a character sits down at a table or takes a drink of a beverage at an important moment.

Parenthetical: A parenthetical describes a specific way of delivering the line for the actor. It is placed directly below the character's name and before the line of dialogue in the script.

The following is a scene from our 6th grade class screenplay *Mountain Dewm[9] (2015)*

```
EXT. SCHOOL CAFETERIA - LUNCHTIME

A 12-year-old boy, DANIEL, sits at a lunch table
enjoying his food with five of his friends: CARSON,
KAI, SAMANTHA, and RUBY.

ASHLEY runs behind DANIEL, catching a football and
throwing it back across the cafeteria area to JAMES.

JIM, an overly excited and obnoxious boy, approaches
the lunch table.

                    DANIEL
          Quick everyone, hide your Twinkies!

JIM sits down at the table uninvited.

                    JIM
          Hey guys, guess what?  I've got a new knock
                    knock joke!

Everyone at the table groans and looks miserable.

                    JIM (CONT'D)
          Knock, Knock.

                    EVERYONE
              (miserable and in unison)
          Who's there?

                    JIM
          Europe.

                    EVERYONE
          Europe who?

                    JIM
          No, YOU'RE a poo!

CARSON laughs and KAI slaps him lightly upside the
```

---

[9] *Mountain Dewm (2015):* https://vimeo.com/129512103

```
          head.  CARSON immediately stops laughing.  Everyone
          else at the table GROANS and shakes their head at the
          bad joke.

          DANIEL reaches into his backpack and pulls out a
          bottle of MOUNTAIN DEW.  He carefully unscrews the
          top.

          ASHLEY catches a pass behind DANIEL.

          DANIEL takes a big gulp of Mountain Dew.  His face
          contorts and he starts to gag and slowly does a face
          plant on the table.

          The expiration date is revealed on the bottle: 3/15/00

          His friends look over at him, worried.

                         JIM (CONT'D)
                    Hey, DANIEL, are you okay?

          DANIEL turns to look at his friend and he blacks out.

          His watch reads 1:03.
```

The screenplay is basic and includes the elements that will be important to the plot. For example, the timing of Ashley and James catching and throwing the football is key to later scenes where there are time travel elements, so their blocking is specifically referenced in the script.

Make Screenplays Available for Students to Read

Most teachers have a classroom library so students can borrow a book to read if there is some down time during the school day. We know much of their growth in spelling and punctuation comes from exposure to the written language: A kid who reads a lot has a bigger vocabulary and higher reading comprehension than a kid who does not. This is also true for learning about story structure and screenplay formatting.

Luckily for us, many of the Pixar screenplays are available online so you can download them and print them out to use as reference. I love Pixar because the films are always school appropriate and they are high interest to any kid at any age. You can also find screenplays for films that are up for screenwriting

Oscars by doing a simple Google search (just be sure the script is school appropriate).

I've downloaded tons of screenplays, printed them out, and put them in small, labeled binders so the kids can take them out and read when there is free time. I also let the kids take the binders outside of class if they want to read them during homeroom or in the evenings. If the pages get torn or the binder gets wrecked, no big deal, I can just print another copy and there are always old binders being thrown away by someone at the school for me to scavenge. Done and done.

Expose Students to Short Films:

For the most part, audiences today don't consume short stories or films. We read 200 page novels or watch 1½ hour-long films or TV shows that carry storylines across 20 episodes. Because of this, students coming into my program typically aren't well versed in the short story genre. They will initially try to emulate what they see in movie theaters or read in novels and this can be frustrating for them when they realize they have bitten off more than they can chew with their story idea.

Unfortunately for us, screenwriting books are written for people who are trying to learn to write and sell feature length films. They're written for people in college and beyond so the content and the films they reference are often not school appropriate or developmentally appropriate for young kids.

The best way to get students familiar with the short film genre is to have them watch and analyze short films. Go on Vimeo or YouTube and search for short films. Show your students Oscar nominated short films or episodes of the Twilight Zone (as appropriate) and analyze their plot as a warm up. Pixar and Disney have been cranking out beautiful shorts to place in front of their animated films and those are absolutely wonderful! I recommend also finding short films made by high school or college students because they will likely be made on a shoestring budget and will feel more relatable to our first time filmmakers.

I teach three types of short films in my classroom:

1. Experimental Short Films:
Experimental Films explore striking visual and artistic ideas. Filmmakers experiment in new ways with every aspect of filmmaking including light, movement, framing, color, and sound. They describe a mood or intellectual idea *instead* of a story.

You've seen these; in fact some of our favorite music videos could be considered experimental films!

Since these films do not tell a traditional story, audiences tend to have a short attention span for them. Young filmmakers should try to keep these films short; less than three minutes is best.

These films are FUN to make with your students!
- Pick a poem or find a piece of music you like and let it inspire you.
- Explore creative lighting, lens flares, and shadows bouncing off of walls.
- Find beautiful shapes in a location and practice some unique camera angles.
- Try out some time-lapse photography, stop motion, and slow motion.
- Use a green screen and try some trick photography.
- Play with movement, blocking, and rhythm in a scene.
- Try some blended edits and edit to the music.

Last school year I had my Visual Effects Lab students create an experimental film. I wanted to give them a ton of opportunities to try out practical and computer visual effects and a traditional narrative film felt like it limited the scope of what I wanted them to accomplish in VFX. Since our only available location was the school, we went with the subject of what it felt like to be a student in middle school. We watched lots of experimental short films, brainstormed ideas, pitched to the class, and we came up with our scenes to shoot. We premiered *School Daze*[10] at our Spring Film Festival and it got a ton of compliments!

It was an absolutely wonderful filmmaking experience for all of us. The kids got to explore their whacky and goofy side and I got to cram a ton of practical and visual effects shots into one project.

2. Sketch/Microshort Films:
A *sketch* is a short film (generally less than 5 minutes in length) with a clear beginning, middle, and end. These stories set up a protagonist that is interesting. The protagonist is placed in a unique situation with a simple goal to achieve. How does it resolve? Do they reach the goal? Do they fail? A sketch can be a comedy, drama, or even a scary film.

---

[10] *School Daze:* https://vimeo.com/219420805

The term "Setup and Punchline" seems to be helpful to my young screenwriters, referring to the telling of a joke. Super simple. Set it up, knock 'em down!

Comedy Examples: Key and Peele, SNL sketches, Superbowl Commercials

Drama Examples: Thai Life Insurance commercials, Google Commercials, Olympics Commercials honoring the athletes

Scary Examples: David Sandberg (username PonySmasher on YouTube) has a ton of microshort horror movies: *Attic Panic* and *Not So Fast* are school appropriate and very effective.

My students love the Sketch format of filmmaking and have done many of them over the years. Last fall my student, Sunny, created a short sketch *iPocalypse*[11] as a social commentary regarding our obsession with cell phones:

Setup: The kids are walking down the street, distracted by their cell phones. They need to pay attention.

Punchline: They all get eaten by zombies and don't notice because they're so distracted by their cell phones.

3. Narrative Short Films:
A *narrative film* is simply a connected sequence of events that is longer than a sketch and is more character driven. Our narrative short films are generally 5-15 minutes in length.

When middle schoolers are writing a narrative screenplay, they need a lot of help to create even the simplest story with a clear beginning, middle, and end. The first time I tried to teach narrative screenwriting, I trotted out the old tried and true "plot mountain" and attempted to have the students write screenplays the same way I was taught to teach narrative writing in my English classes: brainstorm ideas, use graphic organizers to plan details, use a story map to put the events in sequence, then write the first draft. The truth is this just doesn't do enough to help students create consistently strong stories. They were frustrated, their stories were weak, and they kept getting writer's block. In a film class, every student needs to be able to write stories that work every time. In other words: they need to know what makes a good story tick.

---

[11] *iPocalypse:* https://vimeo.com/187702533

A Quick Side Note on Screenwriting for Students of Varying Abilities: The way you present screenwriting as a teacher will depend greatly on how engaged the students are and whether they're ready for this level of independent writing. If they lack engagement or lack ability, you'll need to modify the process so it becomes manageable. I've had classes in the past that need a lot of scaffolding to help them knock together a workable story. The students come up with a crazy idea and I walk them step-by-step through the writing process. One class had many English Language Learners who were very nervous about their ability to read and write in English so our screenwriting process was done orally like a "choose your own adventure" story with the kids brainstorming the possible avenues for the plot and then discussing each one and voting. This is totally okay when you are teaching kids! Their critical thinking is being accessed; so don't beat yourself up if they're not whipping out clever and emotional ten page screenplays all by themselves. It's all about exposure to the process at first.

The next few pages explain exactly how I go at the screenwriting process with my kids. It works for me. Pull from it what works for you.

Writing a Narrative Short Film

Building the Bones of Your Story…it's as easy as 1-2-3!
Have the students answer the following questions in their composition notebooks as they begin to develop their story:

1. Who is my Protagonist?
Describe them! Give them unique qualities so they are memorable. What's in a name? Everything! Some names evoke strong, powerful characters, others are more formal sounding; be sure you choose a name that will help define who your protagonist is.

2. Determine your Protagonist's Wants vs. Needs
What does the protagonist WANT? What is their obvious goal in the story?
Hint: This is usually something fairly simple: *money, the golden treasure, a date to the dance, to win the big game etc.*

What is the protagonist's flaw? (What they NEED is to overcome this flaw!) This flaw should keep them from easily reaching their goal. Make life hard for your protagonist! Personal conflict makes for a more interesting story! (Pay attention! Later, this will become the theme!)
- *Is your movie about a conflict with a bully? Your protagonist could be a coward.*
- *Is your movie about a kid who discovers they can fly? Your protagonist could be afraid of heights.*
- *Is your movie about a kid who wants to win the basketball game? Your protagonist could be unwilling to work as a team because they are selfish and love to show off.*

3. Determine your Ending
Before you begin to write your screenplay, you *must* figure out where your story is going! Have the students briefly free write four possible conclusions for their story based on the 4 Types of Endings:

The 4 Types of Endings:

1. Positive- The protagonist gets what they want AND what they need.

The protagonist reaches their goal AND fixes their character flaw. (This can feel super cheerful. It is wonderful for movies written for small children. Example: *most Disney/Pixar films, It's a Wonderful Life*)

2. Positive Irony- The protagonist doesn't get what they want BUT they get what they need (which is more important anyway, so they're happy).

41

The protagonist does not achieve their goal, but they fix their character flaw along the way. This gives the audience the sense that while the goal wasn't reached, the protagonist is a better person for trying. (This feels like real life- people LOVE this! See: *Dead Poets Society, Rocky, Bruce Almighty*)

3. Negative Irony- The protagonist gets what they <u>want</u> BUT they do not get what they <u>need</u>.

The goal is achieved, but the protagonist doesn't fix their character flaw and therefore isn't a better person for their efforts. The victory feels a little empty for the audience. (NOTE: This can work well in a comedy. Example: *Dumb and Dumber, Denial*[12])

4. Negative- The protagonist doesn't get what they <u>want</u> AND they do not get what they <u>need</u>.

The goal is not achieved and the protagonist does not fix their character flaw. This tends to be a movie with an unsatisfying and sad ending. (Example: *August: Osage County, Anna Karenina*)

Positive: + Character gets what they *want*. + Character ALSO gets what they *need*.	Positive Irony: - Character does *not* get what they want. + Character gets what they need.
Negative Irony + Character gets what they *want*. - Character does *not* get what they need.	Negative: - Character does *not* get what they want. - Character does *not* get what they need.

Have the students put a star next to their favorite ending. Now that they have the beginning and ending of their short film we need to work on the fun, part: creating the juicy details!

---

[12] *Denial*: https://vimeo.com/201572275

Fleshing Out the Story...

Now that your students have the bones of their story, it's time to flesh it out! Many screenwriters like to put the main beats (important moments that move the story forward) onto notecards or post-it notes and arrange them on a wall. If you are working as a class to write a screenplay, this can be a great way to have the students visualize the plot of the film!

One of the oldest pieces of advice about story structure from an unknown source claims: "Act 1: Get the protagonist up a tree. Act 2: Throw rocks at them. Act 3: Get them down from the tree." You might also run across the "Hero's Journey" structure by Joseph Campbell which I find way too complex and difficult to adapt to the short film structure for my young students. I really do like the simple outline structure of *Save the Cat* by Blake Snyder (a *great* read), but again it is intended for writing a feature length screenplay and not short films.

Here's my way of teaching short story structure: Give the students 30 notecards each and using the story outline they just created in their composition notebooks, have them write down the main beats of the story, one on each notecard.

Side Note: If students are working on this at home, encourage them to build a music playlist of songs that feel like they represent the tone of the story and listen to the playlist as they work through this aspect of the writing process.

1. Establishing Beats
(3-5 Note Cards)

What is a beat? For our purposes in screenwriting: **a beat is a unit of action that helps move the story along.**

<u>**Establishing Beats**</u> are events that happen early in the story to **introduce your protagonist and the world they live in.**

<u>**Protagonist:**</u> The main character in a story. Sometimes as simple as "the hero" or "the good guy" but often can be deeply flawed. The story revolves around the protagonist who will usually learn a life lesson through the events of the story.

Let the audience get to know the protagonist by showing them in action! Are they at Home? School? Work? Out with Friends? Give them something to do in their introduction that lets us know what kind of person they are and what they love to do!

Remember! Your protagonist is NOT perfect! Be sure to include a beat or two that establishes their FLAW. (Students have figured this out already in their pre-writing. Have them look back in their notes!)

2. Catalyst
(2-3 Note Cards)

Here is where the conflict occurs that introduces the goal. This moment is always called *the Catalyst* and will introduce us to the *antagonist*. Be sure the goal can't be ignored and is important to the protagonist.

The Catalyst: The event that introduces the conflict. How do you write a great catalyst? Make sure it is a problem that will be difficult for your protagonist to solve. It should be something they care about personally. *Hint: Sometimes the most interesting story starts with a problem that seems insignificant to everyone BUT the protagonist!*

The Antagonist: The character that causes conflict for the protagonist. Sometimes as simple as "the villain" or "the bad guy" but can often be well intentioned. The best villains don't know they are the "bad guy" and are simply acting in their own best interest! (Think: Mother Gothel from *Tangled*.)

3. Off to Pursue the Goal
(5-7 Note Cards)

This is the start of the second act (page 3-4 of a 10 page script). The protagonist is pursuing their goal. What do they do to solve the problem? Often, this is the part of the story where the protagonist goes through training of some kind. *At this point it looks like the hero will overcome their obstacle and reach their goal...until...*

4. Raising the Stakes
(5-7 Note Cards)

The journey gets harder for the protagonist and things start to fall apart. Perhaps problems arise in their circle of friends. While training for the race, the hero suffers an injury. The antagonist (bad guy) figures out what the hero is up to and makes things difficult. In other words: *it looks like the goal may not be easily reached.*

5. All Is Lost
(3-5 Note Cards)

This is the start of the third act and will occur roughly on page 7-8 of a 10 page script. Something happens and the protagonist believes there is no way they can win. *They are giving into despair...when...*

6. Conclusion - "One Last Shot"
(3-5 Note Cards)

Something happens and the protagonist gets one last shot at their goal! It could be a pep talk from a mentor, an ally shows up, they remember advice given to them previously that only now makes sense. Remember! We love to see the protagonist summoning one final moment of courage to defeat the enemy or solve the problem. Your audience would feel massively cheated if Rocky's opponent in the ring dies of a heart-attack right before the end of the match. Why? Because we yearn to see Rocky pull himself up and resolve to triumph courageously over his opponent!

The protagonist either overcomes or is overcome. (Remember: You've chosen your ending already!) Is it satisfying for Rocky to lose the match but get the girl because he is now confident? Sure! (This is the positive irony ending.)

7. Wrap It Up
(3-5 Note Cards)

Tie up loose ends. Make sure the protagonist touches base with the important characters they have interacted with throughout the story. Show your audience how their relationships are different now that the protagonist has overcome their flaw, or reinforce that the flaw remains (negative or negative irony ending).

Arrange the Notecards and Tweak the Events!

Have your students take all of the notecards and arrange them in chronological order for the story. Add, change, modify, throw away, replace, and shuffle until they have between 20-25 cards.

Many professional screenwriters will tape the notecards to the wall or use a huge bulletin board as they rearrange them to help map out their story. Try it!

Drum Roll Please....

NOW you can write the Screenplay!

Use screenwriting software such as Final Draft, Celtx, or Adobe Story if you have it, or use basic word processing software if you don't. Refer the students back to the screenwriting handout if they have questions about formatting.

Writer's Block?

Are the kids getting stuck in a no-end plot or unable to think of unique characters? Maybe they just look at you and shrug miserably when you ask them how it's going. Seek out The 22 Rules of Storytelling according to Pixar. You'll find it online and many people have even done little slide shows with images from Pixar movies to accompany each rule. Go over each rule with the class and discuss examples they can think of in movies they've seen. It's a nice way to unstick your class and get the creative juices flowing again if they're having some trouble.

Help! We're Still Stuck!

Remind students to not be shy about ripping open their story and shuffling ideas or deleting some of their favorite scenes *just to see if it works better*. The term in screenwriting is "kill your darlings." I don't use that particular phrase with the kids; it seems kind of harsh. Instead I remind them to put their favorite scenes that need excising into a writer's notebook to be used for another movie later on. I tell them, "This is a great scene…for some other movie."

If your kids are still stuck go over these helpful tips:

1. Make this the most significant day of your character's life.
   Otherwise your movie might be boring. Yikes!

2. Start at the last possible moment, end at the first possible moment.
   We don't need to see the protagonist wake up, brush their teeth, walk down the hall, eat breakfast etc. *If it has nothing to do with moving the plot forward, cut it!*

3. Make sure your protagonist makes at least ONE hard decision.
   We want to see them take a risk, especially one that will help them fix their character flaw!

4. No flashbacks, dream sequences, title cards, or voice-overs!
   These are crutches that help fix lazy storytelling and break the flow

of your finished film. Have a title card that reads "Two Days Later..."? You shouldn't need to resort to this! If you feel like you want to put one in, go back into your story and ask yourself, *"Can this be fixed so I don't need it?"*

5. Short Film = Short Time Frame

Stay away from epic stories that take place across many years and many locations. You are not making these movies right now! If you have a story to tell and it starts to turn into a massive "Star Wars" – like epic, consider telling *one day* in the life of *one character* from your story or shelving the story for when you have $150 million dollars and the green light from Universal Studios. Trust me.

6. First Impressions

Give your characters an action they can do when they are first introduced in the film that defines who they are and what they're about. It can be an action as subtle as re-organizing a perfectly organized bookshelf to define them as an overly fastidious person. No joke, this is the *best* way to introduce your characters and establish the tone for the film. Not sure what the character should do? There's your problem! You need to know your characters better! Write out their backstory!

7. Backstory Study

Put your screenplay aside and write down a ½ page backstory for your protagonist, antagonist, and secondary characters. See if there is an opportunity to slip some aspect of their backstory into your screenplay. Even if it is small, it will go a long way to make your story more interesting!

8. Focus on Action

Is there a section of your screenplay in which two characters are talking and giving really important information and you're worried it's going to bore your audience? Give your characters something interesting to do during this conversation that will keep the audience's interest until the conversation is finished. *While discussing the plan to trap the leprechaun in the cage, the characters stand in front of a mirror putting on camouflage paint and testing the spring on the cage trap door.*

9. Kill the Unnecessary Dialogue!

"Hi, how are you?" "I'm fine." is a scene killer. Take out all boring and unnecessary dialogue. Get right to the point, or start the scene part way into a conversation! We don't need to see all of the characters walking up to and greeting each other every time there is a new scene!

10. Finished? Think Again!

Think you're finished? Nope! Have someone you trust read your screenplay and give you notes. If they say they have no notes then they are not being helpful; get another opinion! Rewrite!

Chapter 4: Handling Auditions

When a middle school film class needs an actor, it's best to have the actor come from within the class. Why? Because the students will become better directors if they understand what it feels like to be on the other side of the camera. How does a young filmmaker learn to work with actors? By knowing first hand what their concerns are when they step on set.

Step 1: Announce the Auditions
The week before the acting auditions, print out a page from the script that has a pivotal scene for the main characters and pass it out to all of the students regardless of who is interested in auditioning. This should be a scene in which the two lead actors interact in a meaningful way. What we really want is to see how the actors play off of each other. The kids in your class will no doubt have pre-conceived notions about an "audition." Nobody likes to audition in front of their peers and potentially be declined the role. In middle school many kids choose not to audition at all for fear of failure. That's okay. Not everyone has to audition but everyone in the class will be a part of the audition process.

Step 2: Auditions
On the day of the auditions remember to keep a positive atmosphere and applaud any child who steps forward to audition. How do we do this in a class of middle schoolers who tend to be judgmental? Easy! Use the audition process to help your class hone the characters. The kids who are auditioning will be bringing their ideas about the character to the table through their performance. During each audition, the teacher should read the subsequent characters and stage directions. Have the class write down three things the actor did that worked well or helped defined the character in a new way. After every audition, the have the students raise their hands to share their notes and create a master list of all of the positive aspects of the performance. As students get comfortable with the audition process, I get more and more kids raising their hands and wanting to audition too because they see that it is fun and not competitive.

Step 3: Mix and Match the Actors
After everyone has had a chance to audition, mix and match the actors and have them perform together to see if there are actors who have unique or really exceptional chemistry. The kids like this step because they are able to modify their performance as they play off of the other actors in the scene. It becomes much less about one person delivering lines to a group of people and more about interacting with the other actors and getting lots of positive feedback from their friends in the class. Again, the audience needs to write

down three aspects of each performance that worked or added something new to the scene.

Step 4: You Cast the Film
Take a long look at the master lists of comments for each actor. Take the comments into consideration, then remember: *your classroom is not a democracy.* The class will not be voting on which kid should get the part. It does not matter how mature the class is, voting on the actors will only ever be a popularity contest and allow the people voting to feel superior to the people auditioning and that is a *bad idea.* Tell the kids that you are really excited about what you've seen and roles will be posted the following day. NO VOTING!

So how do I cast the class films? First, I take into consideration the performances. The notes from the class are always dead on and if there were any true difficulties with the performance I keep it in mind. I do not give critical feedback on the auditions. It is totally unhelpful to tell a child who auditions that they gave a really wooden performance or should have memorized their lines. This is not a drama class and it is not necessary for me to go down that rabbit hole with them.

Second, I take into consideration the child's attendance record. If they miss a lot of school then it would severely damage production to allow them to be a lead actor in one of our films even if they gave a great performance. I had an actor once miss so much school that we had to turn our class film into a trailer for the film festival. It was a total letdown even though the kid was a brilliant actor.

Third, I take into consideration the chemistry between the actors. There are times when we have one kid who is really strong but two other kids simply vibe well together in the scene. I'd rather have great chemistry than one super strong performance and awkward chemistry.

Fourth, I take into consideration the fact that I want all kids to have a shot at being an actor for one of our films. If there is a super strong actor on the fall semester film, I will generally try to give the big roles to other students on the spring semester film. Remember: this is supposed to be a learning process and the student who is an actor is therefore not available on set to learn how to operate the boom mic or lighting equipment.

Heads Up: When the kids go off to make their own independent film projects, they will need actors too. Most of the time they will use their friends and family as actors, but as they get better and better they will start looking for really good actors. Be careful that they don't hold their own acting auditions as this causes way too much drama and hurt feelings at the middle school level. It is my policy that my students are not allowed to hold acting auditions, period. I tell them that until they can afford to pay their actors union wages for their work, it is unacceptable to ask them to audition. I tell the kids to scout out the school plays and talk with the drama teacher regarding the casting of their film. If they need a kid who can pull off slapstick comedy, the drama teacher will be able to give them a few names and then they can see who might be interested. If they go to the school plays, it will be obvious which kids might be able to handle the role and they should respectfully ask them if they might be interested in working on their film project.

Chapter 5: Assembling Your Film Crews

At this point you should be ready to assemble student film crews and look towards scheduling your film shoot. Start the process by discussing the basic jobs on a professional film set. The students should see what the job looks like in the professional world compared to what the job looks like on your class film set. It's important for the kids to know that on a studio movie as the budget grows the crew grows and jobs get more and more specific. We have a budget of zero dollars; therefore, we do not have the benefit of hiring people or having large crews. For my middle school students I introduce the following positions:

Producer
The producer is the "responsible one" who oversees the project from start to finish and makes sure it does not stray from the original vision.

Producers hire the crew, arrange for locations, make sure all equipment is being rented, casts and finds actors, sets the shooting schedule, coordinates all departments, supervises the script during filming to make sure scenes are shot, and acts as a creative consultant for the director.

Producers on Our Set: I am the producer. I make sure everybody is running on schedule and getting the shots we need. I make sure that if everybody is not on task during our shoot I will find somewhere else for them to be (probably in the Dean's office writing a letter of apology). If a director, sound person, or grip is doing a particularly good job, I take notice! They will be given more opportunities on our film as they come up!

Director
The director is the person responsible for taking the script and deciding how it will be seen on the big screen. The director hires actors, decides on locations, plans the shots before filming begins. On set, the director is in charge of making sure the actors and crew are clear about their jobs, sets up shots, and keeps the movie on schedule and on budget.

Directors on Our Set: The director is the person responsible for taking their assigned scene and planning how it will be filmed. They make a shot list in the right hand margin of their shooting script to make sure we get basic coverage of the scene. They must work with the props and wardrobe department to make sure all props and wardrobe are ready to go for the shoot. They direct the actors' performances and listen to the actor's ideas while making sure we keep in mind the original tone of the movie. They are responsible for making sure the camera is returned to the classroom at the end of the shooting day.

Sound

The Production Sound Mixer records sound during filming. The Boom Operator handles the microphone and boom pole to get clean sound by keeping it as close to the actors as possible without letting it get into the frame.

Sound on Our Set: Our Sound Person has to do the job of both the sound mixer and the boom operator on our set. They do a sound check at the beginning of the shot to make sure the actor's dialogue will be cleanly recorded. They check for noise before a take begins and may delay shooting if there is an airplane in the audio that will be problematic. During a take, they get the microphone as close to the actor as possible without getting it in the shot. Using the headphones they monitor (listen) to the sound being picked up with the microphone to make sure it's clear and loud enough.

Hint: Do a mini-lesson on monitoring audio. What is stereo? Why do we record on set in mono? How loud is loud enough? There are complex answers to these questions, but for the sake of simplicity and being able to move forward, I tell the kids: 1. Record your audio in mono 2. Have your actor say the loudest part of the scene for a test and make sure that bit of audio goes into the yellow *but avoid the red area of the audio level monitor at all costs.* I show them the red button on our audio monitor that tells us when the audio is clipping and I tell them that if it goes into the red, they have broken the audio signal on the way into the camera and it is unfixable in post-production. You cannot fix broken audio by making it softer in your editing program. Is this the whole story about audio? Nope. It's what my kids can handle at this point in their filmmaking careers. I could talk to them about limiters and compressors, but their brains would hurt and they would feel intimidated. Simple advice to young filmmakers: Audio levels should be in the upper green and into the yellow but avoid RED like the plague.

Heads Up: This is the one position that is very difficult to supervise as a teacher on set. You have to have faith in the student to call out any problems they are having with the audio. I can't tell you how many times I double checked that the microphone was on, the levels looked good, and then the student with the boom pole smacked the mic into a tree branch during a scene (over and over) or somehow messed with the gain and we either had damaged audio that was too loud or audio that was unusable because the signal was too low. I've had kids not tell the crew that the helicopter overhead was a problem and because we were all dealing with the craziness on set, nobody noticed and the audio was unusable.

Put your most trusted student in this position or you will regret it in post-production. It is easy to check if the director got all of the shots needed and if the performances were clean enough to move on, but it is almost impossible as the teacher to know if there were problems with the audio on the set.

Lighting

Lighting a scene helps highlight a great performance in your actors and show off your wonderful locations and set design.

Mini Lesson: Three Types of Lighting:
1. The Key Light: Located on the front and slightly to the side of the setup to cast a bright light on one side of the frame while leaving shadow on the other side (to be filled in later).
2. The Fill Light: Used to fill in the shadowy areas of the key light. It is usually less intense or can even another color than the key light to change the effect.
3. Back Light: Light shining on the back portions of the subject so we can see three dimensions.

On a professional set, the Director of Photography or Cinematographer is responsible for making sure each set is lit correctly for the tone of the scene. There are many different types of lights used and they often will have a crew of gaffers or electricians to help set up and sculpt the light to create the best effect.

Lighting on Our Set: When we shoot outside, our key light will be the sun. Our fill light will be the sun bouncing off of a reflector (or bounce board). The crewmember in charge of lighting will be responsible for arriving to the set quickly and figuring out where the sun is in relation to our actors and what is needed in terms of shade or bounced lighting. During each scene, they must manage the lighting so it is stable. Remember: bounce boards are flimsy and can potentially shake if there is wind.

If we shoot indoors, lighting is fairly simple using the overhead lights. Often we can add some practical lights to add effect: examples might be a lamp at a desk, a lighted fish tank, a lava lamp in a science classroom, or garland lights across a bulletin board.

Grip

The Grip is responsible for setting up the equipment and getting the set ready for filming. The grip works with the Director of Photography to put up and test the lights, and makes sure all electric components are plugged in to a working source of electricity. If there are camera moves, the Grip is responsible for setting up the crane or dolly and track for filming.

A Grip On Our Set: The grip brings out the tripod and other camera attachments and gear and prepares the set for filming. If something needs to be moved or changed at the location, the grip oversees this. For example, if the picnic tables in the cafeteria need to be moved or wiped down in the morning because they are covered in dew, the grip oversees the entire class in moving or wiping down the tables with paper towels.

Props and Wardrobe
On a large production, there are many people responsible for props and wardrobe. Their job is to make sure all props are found, created, built, labeled, and organized for the days shoot. Their job is also to keep an eye on continuity so everything matches within each scene.

Props and Wardrobe on Our Set: The Props and Wardrobe Department makes a list of items needed for each scene in the screenplay.

The Wardrobe Department works with each actor to bring in wardrobe options and then work together to decide which wardrobe goes with which scene. If the screenplay covers multiple days, they organize the wardrobe so the actor knows which items to wear for each day.

The Props Department builds or finds props and makes note of which props are needed for each scene being shot. Each shooting day, they are responsible for having the correct props accounted for and ready to go.

Heads Up: Middle schoolers are NOT naturally good at this. It's fun to build the one "special" or "cool" prop, but the day-to-day boring props will be forgotten and then you'll go insane trying to find the one prop needed for the scene you are currently shooting. Your actor will inevitably forget which item of wardrobe they are supposed to be wearing for which scene. The fix? Stick a piece of tape onto each item of wardrobe with the scene numbers that item will be used in. Keep a props box with a label that itemizes all of the props and make sure your wardrobe and props department doesn't leave class at the end of a shooting day until all props are accounted for and all wardrobe is back where it belongs and labeled. Also, make life easy on yourself and have the actors wear jeans for every scene in the shoot. It takes a lot less time for the kids to run to the bathroom and change their shirt or simply pull a sweater over their head than it does to run to the bathroom and change all of their clothes. Time is sanity; don't let it get away from you!

Continuity/Script Supervisor
The script supervisor oversees continuity on set. They will keep track of wardrobe, props, hair, and the blocking of a scene. If an actor says a line then raises a glass and takes a drink; it is the script supervisor's job to make a note of that and remind them to do it the same way for the rest of the takes in the scene.

Continuity/Script Supervisor on Our Set: This crewmember takes a picture of the set with their cell phones (double check that it is okay to do that at your school). This way when we need to go back to the beginning of the scene, we know exactly where all of the props were and how the wardrobe looked. Was the pencil at the top of the desk, or in the actor's hand? Was the actor's collar up or down? Was their hair over their shoulder or tucked behind their ear?

Production Assistant
The Production Assistant is always ready to perform all types of chores from traffic control to taking messages between departments and managing food service for the cast and crew. PA's are often right out of film school and looking to get some experience by working and observing on the set.

A Production Assistant on Our Set: Everyone on our set is a Production Assistant. We are all trying to get a film made and we have very little time to shoot. If someone needs help with something, everyone must help. It is *everyone's* job to get the production rolling. My policy to the students is: IF you feel you are doing more work than anyone else, please write the producer (Ms. Bennett) a formal letter explaining your concerns and give it to her after class. (Since Ms. Bennett is not just a producer, but a PA as well, she will be too busy to hear you complain until the end of the period.)

Heads Up: It is important to make sure all of the kids are willing to pitch in and no one feels "above" anyone else. If the kids see you the teacher wiping off a grimy lunch table so the kids can sit on it and you ask for help, they will likely pick up a paper towel and join in. Make sure as you're wiping if you see the director standing around not doing anything, you get them to help you wipe down the table too.

Storyboard Artist
A storyboard artist works during pre-production to break down a scene by sketching frames showing camera angles to be shot in order to help the director better visualize the scene.

Storyboarding On Our Set: For those students who do not have an acting or crew position on that particular day of shooting, I have them sit off camera and storyboard each shot we are filming in their composition notebooks. After we shoot the scene, if there is time, I will ask the class if they have any suggestions for "What if we?" shots. This is my own term for angles or shots that are not part of basic coverage but could add interest to the scene that we hadn't thought of before. The kids who are storyboarding have lots of time to sit and contemplate the scene, so we actually get the best ideas from them! The next day I check their notebooks and give them a class participation grade for their work.

Do we need all of these positions? Should we have others?
The positions on your film set can vary depending on what your project is and what your goals are for the students. If you are making a silent film, you won't need someone on set for sound. If you're making a music video you probably won't need a sound person but you will likely need a person designated for playback so your performers will have the music to hear as they are dancing or lip-syncing during the shoot.

If you have a lot of students, maybe you'll want to provide more jobs. If your students are not confident filmmakers, maybe you'll want to have fewer jobs.

Jobs can also be combined. For example, if you only need a tripod for the scene, then the grip can set it up then jump over to working with the bounce board for lighting.

The Bottom Line: Make sure every student has something they are responsible for on set. Remind them that the crew positions change each semester and they will learn a new job on the next film. Also remind them the point of a class film is for the kids to learn how to behave on a film set so when they make their own films they will be efficient and get the most out of the shoot.

Crew Letters of Request:
When you've gone over all of the jobs on set, have the students write you a formal letter requesting one of the crew positions and explaining why they are interested in that job. My kids typically will write one full page for their Crew Letter of Request. The kids who write thoughtful letters get priority over students who don't. If I have someone who is upset over not being chosen to be the sound person or the director, I can always go back to their letter of request and tell them they need to put more thought into applying for the job next time. It's in their hands and it's not about me picking favorites.

Divide Up The Work
At this point I assign a full crew to each scene of the film. Because we have

large class sizes, there is a different director, sound person, lighting person, and grip for each scene. Remember: the point of making this film is for the students to learn how to conduct work on a set and how each job fits into the bigger picture within production. Would you get a better movie made if you had only one kid direct and one kid do sound? Yes, no doubt, but the point is to get a class of 40 students to learn how to be filmmakers, so they all need a chance to participate on set.

Chapter 6: Pre-Production Crew Meetings

Once you have sorted the kids into their production crews, they need to take time as a crew to talk through their scene and make a shot list of the basic coverage they'll need. To keep everything simple, I have the kids write the shot list in the right hand margin of their screenplays in pencil (in case they need to erase).

At this point I will also do mini-lessons with the grips, lighting, and sound departments to give them a chance to work with the equipment and ask any questions they might have.

Wardrobe and props crewmembers will make a list of every prop mentioned in the script and make notes on wardrobe. For example, if the script says the protagonist sits down at a desk and pulls their hoodie over their head, then the wardrobe makes note of that.

When each group has their pre-production work finished, we walk through the screenplay again, reviewing the shot list, equipment, wardrobe, and props as a class making sure nothing was missed.

Any shots or sequences that are really complex or need to be shot for VFX work later on should be storyboarded. Keep it simple. Use stick figures and notate beneath the frame any information that will be helpful for the shot. I have the kids draw these storyboards on the back of their screenplays. Having them draw a shot list or storyboard on a separate piece of paper, even if it is in a notebook, becomes confusing and winds up being lost or not used on set. Best to keep everything together in the script.

If you have any VFX shots at this point you'll need to take a few days to do a test shot and show the students the elements of the shot needed to composite later on. This is an excellent opportunity to show them why you must never bump a camera or tripod when shooting a clean plate for a background in a VFX shot.

All of these steps should be modified depending on your students' ability levels. You know best what they can handle. This is a very complex way to run a classroom, so cut yourself some slack on your first few films.

In 2008 for our summer film *Dreamer*, the director's big goal was to learn how to shoot a fight sequence. We knew that would mean lots of different camera angles and I figured it would be smart to have Cameron storyboard the entire fight scene. He hates drawing, but I insisted and somehow in the craziness of pre-production and production, things got so busy that I never actually saw the storyboards.

Four years later, Cameron and I were sitting together on another movie set...

"Hey, kiddo, remember when I had you storyboard that action sequence for *Dreamer*?"

"Yeah, that was hideous."

"But the fight scene looked beautiful, so it was worth it, right?"

"Do you know how many storyboards I created for that one scene?"

"About 15-20?"

"200."

"What?"

"200. My hand cramped up. It took me two days."

I thought about my little 13-year-old Cameron on that film slogging through 200 storyboards because his teacher told him to. Cameron has near photographic memory and legitimately didn't need to create 200 storyboards for the sequence. A shot list in the margins would have been sufficient. Luckily we were able to laugh long and hard about it.

The Lesson? Keep an eye on your kids so you really get a good idea what they actually need in terms of their shot list and storyboards. It is going to be different for every kid and every class.

Chapter 7: Production

Some of our class films were shot during the school day; others were shot on a Saturday when we had more time and fewer distractions. The goal for me is always to make the film curriculum work during class time because as much as possible I want my weekends to be devoted to family time, laundry, and grocery shopping. If you want to shoot a film during the school day, here is what I suggest:

Organizing Your Day:
Remember: you have no time to waste on a shooting day. None. While I want the kids to do all of the work themselves, there are a few things I do as a teacher before the kids walk into the classroom:
- ✓ Write on the board the names of crew and actors required for the scene you will be shooting.
- ✓ Double check that the camera has full batteries and backup batteries.
- ✓ Make sure the SD cards have been initialized/reformatted.
- ✓ Double-check the camera settings: frame rate, audio inputs, etc.
- ✓ Are they shooting outside? Slap on a polarizing lens filter to cut glare.

But shouldn't they be responsible for checking on this stuff as good practice? Yep! Do all of the above and then have them double check and re-initialize when they walk into the classroom. This way if they accidentally skip a step, it doesn't leave the class with unusable footage. You've got to walk a narrow line between letting them do all the work and making sure they get usable footage so your entire film doesn't derail and require tons of frustrating reshoots.

When the kids arrive: *Try to do all of the following in five minutes:*
- ✓ Take attendance
- ✓ Send actors to the bathroom to change into wardrobe
- ✓ Props crew locates the props for the scene
- ✓ Grip unpacks the tripod
- ✓ Director unpacks the camera
- ✓ Sound person gathers the boom mic, XLR cable, and headphones
- ✓ Lighting person unpacks the bounce board
- ✓ The rest of the class takes a composition notebook and a pencil and everyone heads out to the location together.

At the Location:
- ✓ Figure out quickly the general direction of the angles you'll be shooting.

- ✓ Put the class sitting so they can see the set without being in any of the shots.
- ✓ Have the director start blocking the scene with the actors while the grip and lighting crew set up the camera and lighting equipment.

This is where trouble occurs: Perhaps the location is being used by another class for something, a school tour is standing in the middle of your location, a room you need to shoot in is locked even though you cleared the location with the plant manager earlier in the day, or the picnic table has been pooped on by seagulls. This is where you need your sense of humor and patience. Remember: You have lots of PA's on your set! Send a kid to scout a secondary location, ask the plant manager to open the room, or grab some paper towels.

Working with Actors: On one of our very first film projects we were shooting after school and had an actor playing a secondary role who would take her phone out of her pocket and check her texts in the middle of a scene if she wasn't saying a line. It annoyed me until I realized that it was in fact my fault. This girl didn't know that a large part of acting is what you are doing on screen when another actor has dialogue.

So am I to teach acting too? Yes, a little bit. I am not an actor myself and am horribly uncomfortable being on camera. It's made me more patient with actors who are not comfortable with the job. Due to the immense amount of teaching that goes into making a movie with young students, I tend to keep this simple. If your actor is still looking uncomfortable after the table read the most important thing you can do is keep a supportive atmosphere. Compliment *anything* they are doing well. You cannot fire an actor off of your class film set, so you've got to find a way to make it work. For the most part if you can keep your actors from looking at the camera or the crew, you're off to a good start. Shoot the wide or establishing shots first so the actors can get into their groove (these shots are typically the least used in the final edit so if they screw up or are a bit awkward at first it will not be as damaging to the finished film). The last shots filmed should be the close ups or over the shoulders. At this point, our actors will be at their most comfortable and will give us their best performances. Never let the students or actors see that you are unhappy with what they are doing. In a middle school or high school film you can give the actor a line reading and not have them be insulted. Remember: you have 50 minutes to get to the location, shoot, and pack up. There isn't much time to get the actor warmed up. Just do your best and *keep your sense of humor.*

Heads Up: If the equipment is not working correctly or the kids aren't getting the correct shots, they'll be tempted to say, *"Don't worry, we'll fix it in post."* No you won't. Don't ever say that. Don't let the kids think this is actually a thing that people say on the set of films (even though it is). Bad habit. Stop and address the problem.

Roll Up Your Sleeves, Producer! Kids who are brand new to filmmaking will need you to remind them what to say and where to stand on their film set. The sound person will need you to come over and remind them how to hold the boom pole. The lighting person will need your confirmation that they have positioned the bounce board correctly. The director will likely giggle the first time they call "Action!" because they're uncomfortable. You will literally have to fly to each position and remind them what they are supposed to be doing when action is called. The following year, they will need fewer reminders from you and the year after that they should be independent in their jobs. It all depends how confident the kids are and how well you've taught them before you get to the set.

Every film set is run in a slightly different manner. Do what works best for you. For me, I train the kids to:

1. Get the shot set up
2. The director calls out "Picture's Up!" (This is the cue for all crew to get into position.)
3. The sound person puts the boom into position, checks for shadows, listens for clean audio, and says, "All Clear!"
4. The director presses record and calls, "Rolling Camera!"
5. The director waits ~3 seconds making sure everything is recording then calls, "Action!"
6. When the scene is finished, the director yells "Cut!"
7. The director waits 2-3 seconds and then stops recording.

Frustrating On Set Behavior: While the camera is rolling I've noticed several annoying habits that seem to be universal to new filmmakers:
1. In a static shot they will put their hands on the camera and adjust the framing in the middle of a take. *(Stop. Touching. The. Camera!)*
2. They will often cut a scene short yelling, "Cut!" right after the last line of dialogue is spoken. *(Let the scene end naturally!)*
3. They have a tendency to yell cut and press the stop record button at the same time. *(That little bit of extra footage at the end of a take is priceless in the editing room.)*

With 10 Minutes Left: Have the class end the shoot even if they didn't quite get everything they wanted. Don't allow them the bad habit of shooting until the bell rings and asking for a late pass to their next class. Learning how to shoot and scoot in this way takes time and packing up the equipment is every bit as important as what the kids are doing on the set.

- ✓ Make sure the cables are wrapped and put away properly.
- ✓ Make sure the tripod is back in its case with the plate on.
- ✓ Make sure the camera is put away with the lens cap on.
- ✓ Make sure the bounce board is folded and put away.
- ✓ Make sure the wardrobe and props are returned and accounted for.

The Teacher Isn't Finished:
At this point you're going to feel like you got hit by a steam roller and you'd like nothing more than to put your head down and sleep at your desk. Nope. Immediately transfer the footage from the SD card onto your computer. If your footage needs to be transcoded, do it immediately after the day of shooting. Log the footage by scene so that it is quickly accessible to the students while they are editing. At this point you will notice if there were any problems with the footage and can begin to plan for reshoots or work-arounds.

File Sizes:
On a professional film, the workflow is much different from a middle school class film. Make sure the footage will fit onto the hard drives of the students' computers for editing. I'd love to edit in 4K but our classroom computers don't have the storage or speed. I tend to give the kids Apple ProResLT footage.

The Day After Shooting:
The students who storyboarded the previous day in their composition notebooks need to show you their work for credit (just walk around the room and check it off quickly at the start of the period while they're doing their warm up). Go through the footage and discuss the really positive things you saw going on during the shoot. As you go through the footage, you can even tag the clips that are really great so the kids can start with those clips when they begin editing. At the end of the period, quickly review what you will be shooting the following day and which crew is on deck.

Chapter 8: Editing

A Note on Editing Software:
In my classroom we use Apple computers with Adobe Creative Cloud software. I've used all of the major editing programs at some point in my life and have settled on Adobe Premiere in my classroom for a few reasons:

1. It works equally well on both PCs and Macs so the kids who have PCs at home can purchase the relatively cheap software and not miss a beat when working on their homework projects after learning editing techniques in my classroom.

2. The Adobe Creative Cloud is an awesome deal. A Creative Cloud subscription gives you every one of Adobe's applications that you can download and use with free updates. My students are constantly using Adobe Premiere, After Effects, Media Encoder, Audition, and Photoshop for their homework projects so this is a great deal.

3. Adobe Premiere is user friendly and since we also use the other Adobe applications in the classroom, the interfaces on the programs are so similar it makes going between them a snap especially with the "Adobe Bridge".

4. Adobe Premiere is used by professionals. *Spider-Man Homecoming, The Social Network, Deadpool,* and *Hail Caesar* were all edited on Adobe Premiere. What the kids learn in my classroom will last them a very long time if they continue to make movies.

5. If your school has a computer lab, you may very well have a site license for the Adobe Creative Cloud so you won't have to pay for it through fundraising.

Some film teachers love iMovie, some love Final Cut Pro, others will use Avid Media Composer and people will get into major online flame wars about which one is better. Ignore the flame wars. Use the program you like the most with your kids.

Step 1. Logging the Footage
Remember: The workflow for a professional editor is not going to work for your classroom. Using metadata to log footage is going to confuse the kids at this age who are learning as a class (although go for it if you're teaching high school or college students). If the files are not already in a quicktime readable format (if they are .mxf files for example) you should transcode them to .mp4

or .mov files so kids can quickly open them from the desktop to look through the takes.

Kids need consistency in file organization and labeling, so log the footage in the following way *every time*:

On the desktop keep separate folders for each class (do not lock the folders because it will cause trouble with the editing program later on).

Example:
Desktop -> 6th Grade CAAM (folder) -> Movie Title (folder) -> Scene 1 Lockers (folder) -> MVI_2133.MOV (footage)

I label each folder with the scene number first, then a one-word location description. This way the folders are in scene order and are easier to manage.

The footage directly from the camera will be automatically labeled in chronological order by take so students should be able to find the footage easily if it is in folders that are labeled by scene number.

After all of the footage is "in the can" and you've organized your folders, you'll need to transfer the files onto the computers in your classroom so the kids can edit. Depending on the size of your classroom computer hard drives, you may need to transcode the footage to a smaller file size. (Again, I use Apple ProResLT for our files and transcoding is done quickly through Adobe Media Encoder.)

Step 2. Teaching the Basics
I allow a few days for my students to look through all of our footage and tag the takes that are the best. They absolutely love doing this and are really curious about what was shot. Allowing this time for the kids to get familiar with the footage really pays off as they get into the technical aspects of editing later on.

To begin editing I have one very simple task (in four parts): 1. Get the students to correctly import the footage into Premiere. 2. Bring the footage into the timeline. 3. Make a few very simple straight cuts. 4. Export the footage correctly. Depending on their familiarity with computers, this may take anywhere from one class period to a week. My incoming students generally need two days: one day to import the footage and learn the basics of the editing interface and another to export the timeline.

You would be shocked at how many kids have trouble with this. Here's the rub: This generation of students grew up with simple apps on their iPads and Smart Phones. They learned to use these apps by clicking around and figuring it out which works great on an iPad but gets you into a huge, hairy mess in a professional editing program. They don't know what all of the different codecs, aspect ratios, bit rates, and file types are for video and audio and if they set up their edit with the wrong sequence information this will come back to bite them in the form of super long renders and crashing exports. Thank you to Adobe for addressing this issue and making it easier with the newer versions of Premiere. The fact remains, however, there are many ways to get in trouble when using super complex editing software.

Two things:
1. Teach them the easiest way to import footage, the correct way to set up their editing timeline, and how to export from the timeline correctly.
2. Do not be surprised when they fail to listen, click blindly around in the program, and have to learn the hard way.

Last year I had a really advanced 3rd year student miss school the day his film project was due. Then he missed the next three days in a row. I called his mom to see if he was okay and she said he had been sitting in front of his computer trying to finish his edit since the previous weekend and it kept crashing on him. She let him stay home because the deadline for a very important high school application was coming up and this film was a major part of the application. I asked if it would be okay for me to come over to their house and see what was going on. I was honestly really worried about his emotional state. She was relieved and invited me right over. I sat down next to him at his computer and asked him to show me what was going on. The poor kid was in a fog of anxiety and frustration.

"I'm sure if I just re-edit the whole thing in a new sequence that I'll be able to export with no problem."

"Kiddo, how many times have you re-edited the footage in a new sequence?"

"I don't know, five or six?" His hands were shaking as he was trying to quickly re-edit all of his footage.

"Stop. Do me a favor. I want you to show me how you start a new sequence."

He had been setting up his sequence with the wrong aspect ratio and wrong frame rate each and every time he had started a new edit. Of course it was gong to crash on export.

67

"Remember when we learned how to set up our sequence with 'New Sequence from Clip'?" I asked quietly.

There was an insane flood of emotion as the kid realized he had done the simplest thing wrong. The most basic step in editing I had taught the kids and reinforced through three years in my class was something he had disregarded in his haste and had caused him four days of missed school, massive panic, and anxiety.

The Good News? He finished the edit, exported it correctly, got the application in, and was accepted to the high school.

The Better News? He will NEVER make that mistake again.

Sometimes they have to learn the hard way.

Example First Lesson on Adobe Premiere (50 minute class period)

Editing Day 1:
Step 1: With the students, open Adobe Premiere

>At the welcome screen **select "New Project"**

>New Project Window *(explain what each section means- the kids will want to just click "OK" but really force them not to do this or they will wind up losing their project when it is saved somewhere randomly on the computer.)*

>>Location -> Browse -> Select Class Folder on Desktop
>>Name: LastNameTitleEdit
>>   (Example: BennettFluSeasonEdit)
>>Click: OK

>You now have a blank Premiere Session in front of you. Walk the students through each window, explaining how the interface works.

Step 2: Import the Footage
>Go to: File -> Import…
>>Locate and Click on the folder inside the class folder with the title of the movie on it.
>>Click "Import"
>>>You will now see the folder in your Project Window.

Step 3: Create a New Sequence
> Scroll Open the Folder with your footage in it.
> Scroll Open Scene 1 and find the first take.
> Drag the first take to the timeline to create your sequence.
>> Adobe Premiere will create a sequence with the aspect ratio, frame rate, bit depth etc. that matches your clip.

This is a good opportunity to show students what happens if they set up their sequence incorrectly. Show them what it looks like when put their 1920x1080 footage into a timeline designed for 720x420. Explain what an aspect ratio is, mathematically.

Step 4: Begin to edit scene 1
- ✓ Show the kids how to double click on the footage in the Project Window to bring it into the Source Window.
- ✓ Select the In point and the Out point in the source window to select the part of the clip they want to work with, then drag the clip to the timeline.
- ✓ Show the kids how to move the clips around on the timeline and explain the selection tool, trim tool, and razor tool. *(Over time you will teach them all of the tools and buttons, but for day one, keep it simple.)*
- ✓ Give them independent time to work with Scene 1 as you circulate through the class answering questions.

Step 5: Export
No, they do not have a finished film but I want them to learn how to export correctly right off the bat anyway. Give yourself plenty of time for exporting. If your computers are slow this could take some time. It is extremely important to teach the kids to properly save, export, and close out of the program so it is not open when the next class comes to edit.

Exporting:

1: Place your play bar on the first frame of your sequence in the timeline and press "I" on your keyboard to mark the Sequence In point.

2: Place your play bar on the last frame of your sequence in the timeline and press "O" on your keyboard to mark the Sequence Out point.

3: Go to: File -> Export -> Media
> At the bottom of the window select: Sequence In/Out (otherwise you will export the entire timeline including all of the empty space)
>> Under Export Settings:
>>> Format: H.264
>>> Preset: Vimeo HD 1080p
>> *You as the teacher should figure out which preset is best based on the footage you*

give your students. I use the Vimeo preset since all of our films end up on our Vimeo Channel.

Output Name: LastNameTitleEdit1
(example: BennettFluSeasonEdit1)

Subsequent edits will then be labeled the same way progressively numbered so it is obvious which edit is the most recent.

Be sure Export Video and Export Audio are both checked.
Leave all other settings and Click "Export"

4: When the export is finished
File-> Save
Premiere Pro -> Quit Premiere Pro

Students can leave when they show me their correctly labeled and exported video in the correct folder on their desktop.

This first day of editing is where I need to go really slowly and remind the students that they are using professional editing software that is used in films they see at the movie theater. Some of my students are immediately comfortable with it, but most are not and become very anxious about working inside Premiere. It can feel like an impossible mountain to climb when they first see all of the symbols, windows, and dropdown menus that they do not understand. I always congratulate them at every step of the way. The first day is hard, but they will gradually build confidence as they become more and more familiar with the program. This confidence is what we need young children to have because it translates into confidence in other areas. A tough math assignment suddenly doesn't look so tough when they remember they are successfully using professional editing software in my class.

Step 3. Mini-Lessons in Editing
Every day I take stock of what is becoming a problem for the kids and do a mini-lesson at the start of class the next day. Some mini-lessons are super short explanations of the different icons, quick keys, and functions within the editing program; others are more involved step-by-step directions for Basic Titles, Cleaning Audio, Audio Compression, Color Correction, Letterboxing, Rolling Credits, Motion Tracking, Green Screen Basics, Time Remapping, and Time-lapse.

The kids have a three ring binder for the class, so when I create handouts for editing they can quickly reference them later. The handouts change every year depending on the needs of the kids, the software updates, and the specific requirements of the films we make as a class.

Example Handout on Titles in Adobe Premiere:

Creating Basic Titles in Adobe Premiere

When you're ready to create a title go to Title -> New Title -> Default Still...

A "New Title" window pops up.
Name your title something obvious (Example: Main Title)
Click "OK"

The Title Window then pops up.
Click and drag the cursor over the area you want to type your title.
Type your title.
Allow the kids time to play around with different fonts and styles.

When you're done, close the window by clicking the red circle in the upper left hand corner of the title window.

Go to the project window (lower left hand corner), find the title that you just created, and drag it to the track above the clip in your timeline where you want it to appear.

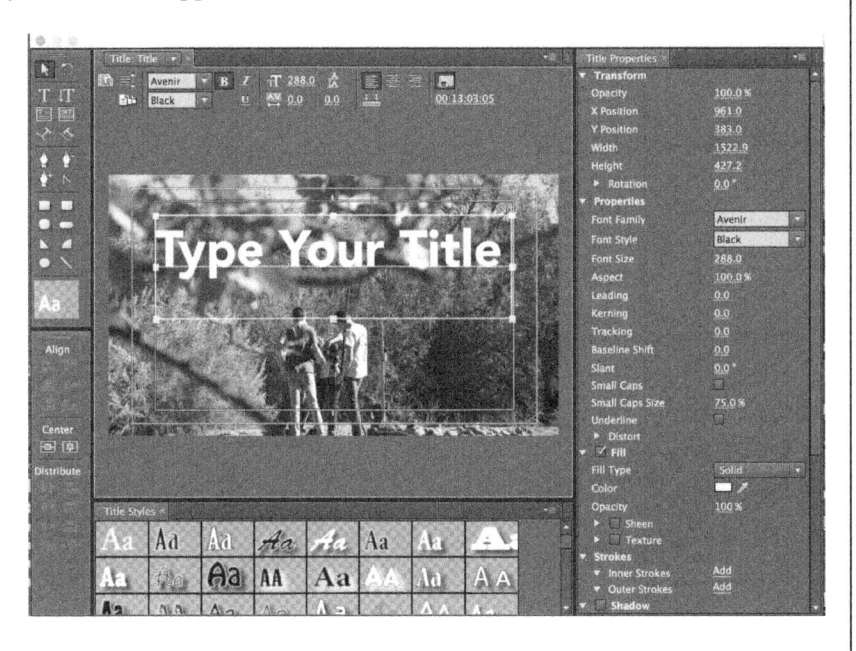

71

Making a Film Look Professional:
A computer teacher friend of mine years ago was teaching his kids PowerPoint. He was tired of the projects that had garish looking titles and the same crummy sound effects and transitions used over and over. The first two days of the next semester, he gave his new class the most horrible task he could think of: Create a PowerPoint Presentation of at least ten slides on any topic using every font, color, sound effect, and transition available in the program. He forced the kids to create the most obnoxious, ugly presentations ever so they could move beyond the novelty of the canned applause sound effect and cutesy hard-to-read fonts. It worked. His kids chilled out after that and started creating professional looking presentations.

In my classroom once the kids get a grasp on the basic editing tools, they'll need time to explore. If you've got super young kids like I do, they'll try to use all of the goofy bells and whistles to show off. If I try to teach them something serious, they'll inevitably distract themselves trying to find out how to create obnoxious looking moving titles, make rainbow colored flashes using the color correction tool, and their favorite: find a frame with an actor looking like they're about to sneeze and freeze frame it with a silly title under it. As a teacher, I have to give them a few days to explore the program and be goofy. I find my happy place and remember: this is the best way for them to learn the program! They're learning what color correction does, how to freeze a frame, and the extreme options available in creating a title. This. Is. A. Good. Thing! If I have time, I give them little silly challenges: Figure out how to make the titles look like they're bouncing around the screen. Figure out how to make the film black and white. Figure out how to freeze frame on a silly looking frame. When a kid figures it out, I give them a small prize (a pencil or a fun eraser or whatever I have on hand) and then tell them to teach the entire class the trick.

This time is where the kids start becoming more confident with the editing program. There is no fear of ruining something important in the edit so they are more likely to try out editing tricks they are unsure of. Ultimately, my students want to create films that look like the professional films they see in the theater. They get a huge rush when someone watches their film and doesn't believe a 12-year-old made it. Just give them a minute to be spazzy with the editing software first.

Chapter 9: Copyright Concerns

I get this a lot from my students: "Ms. Bennett, I know someone who made a video and posted it on YouTube and it was rejected because of the copyrighted music."

Middle school students are not going to have the ability to pay a composer to write original music for their film. As young filmmakers they need to learn how music interacts with the visual elements of a story and the best way to do that is to have them play around with adding music from other films into their own movies. Royalty Free music is great and has come a long way, so if you have access to an account for the kids that could be really helpful. As a film scoring major I really want to encourage the next generation of filmmakers to use music that includes real performances by live orchestras. I want them to have an appreciation for the way a live performance affects the tone and emotion in a film. The best way is to have them listen to and explore the scores of films that were already released. This music is copyrighted, but because my students are still in school and their films are being created for non-profit educational purposes only, the law does offer leeway for students to use copyrighted music under the Fair Use Law.

Please note that I am not a lawyer and Fair Use Laws are subject to change. It is a good idea to research and refresh your understanding of these laws every year.

Under Current Fair Use Law, use of copyrighted material depends on: *"The purpose and character of the use including whether such is of a commercial nature or is for nonprofit educational purposes."*

Under this law your work is evaluated for the following concerns:

#1: The Purpose and Use
Is your video used for education or to make money? Was your video created as an assignment in a school film elective class? For my students their work is purely educational and noncommercial, so it should be okay to use the copyrighted music.

#2. Nature of the Work Used
How is the music being used creatively? Most likely the video uses the music in a new way and is therefore considered "transformative" so it should be okay to use the music in a school film project.

#3. **The Amount of the Work Used:**
Is the music the central focus of your film? If the copyrighted music was not used in its entirety and is not the central focus of the work then it may be okay to use the music for a school film project.

#4. **The Effect of the Use on the Potential Market:**
If the entire song is in your film and people can just download your film instead of purchasing the song then NO, you should not use the music for your film project. If it is only in bits and pieces and is used only to support the filmmaking in certain places then it may be okay to use the music for a school film project.

This being said, remember that a music video or silent film with a song that plays in its entirety would certainly _not_ meet these requirements for "Fair Use".

Film Festivals may try to make money off of your movie by selling tickets to screenings, so they likely will not allow a film with copyrighted music into their festival.

Note: I have had many students *and* parents over the years argue with me that since they purchased a song on iTunes, they now own it and should be able to use it in any way they want. This is not true. A person who purchases a song on iTunes has license to use it only for their own personal entertainment. This does not include re-releasing that song for your own financial gains.

Chapter 10: Every Day Warm Ups

I'm a huge believer in a consistent class structure no matter what the grade level. In a class as complicated as our filmmaking classes, it's important to have the kids approach the subject matter in small bite sized pieces before attempting to pull together an actual film. Warm ups reinforce the language of filmmaking and helps students focus and get their creative juices flowing at the beginning of a class. The only time I don't do a warm up is on a day that we are filming due to time constraints. All warm ups are completed in their Cinematic Arts composition notebook.

Warm Up #1: Recall a Conversation:
Recall a conversation you heard during lunch today and write it in proper screenplay format with scene headings, dialogue, and action.

Why this warm up? This is a very simple way to have your students practice writing in proper screenplay formatting. It is also helpful because young writers struggle with writing realistic dialogue. Trust me, you'll see far too many movies starting with one kid walking up to another kid and saying, "Hi, my name is Alex." Kids don't talk to each other like that in the real world, so having them reflect on their real day-to-day conversations is actually very helpful!

Warm Up #2: Character History:
Show the students a picture of a person (grab one from the internet):
Write a full page in your composition notebook about this person: What is their name? What is their job? What is their biggest accomplishment? What is their goal in life? Who is their best friend? What do they like to do on a Friday night? What is their greatest fear? Give them a character flaw that directly relates to their fear.

You can add your own character questions depending on how much time you allot for the warm up.

Why this warm up? Students tend to write protagonists as bland versions of themselves. Every character is "nice" and "cool" and has a best friend. This is boring to an audience and lacks creativity from the writer. Teaching about idiosyncrasies and character flaws is important and writing unique and flawed but likable characters takes lots of practice!

Warm Up #3: Write a Scene that reflects the TONE of the music:
Give the students 1½-2 minutes of an orchestral film score (not a song): *Listen to the music the first time it is played and then write one scene that reflects the tone of the music in proper screenplay formatting. Remember: a scene is a unit of action taking*

75

place in one location. A movie is made up of many scenes that move the story along, so your scene should be just one moment of a bigger story.

When they read their scene, play the music to go with it!

Why this warm up? One of the hardest things for young filmmakers to learn is the relationship between the story and the music they will eventually need to use in their finished film. Some students will be naturals at finding great music for their movies and others will simply slap into the sound track whatever song is super hot on the radio right now. Great film music tells the emotional story of your film. If you play a piece of score that sounds mysterious and a kid writes a scene about a moonlit cave on the beach with pirates burying treasure; when the scene is read back, the class will suddenly get a very vivid mental picture of the tone of the film. Many writers in Hollywood set up a playlist with music that puts them in the right headspace for their latest script and then listen to that play list over and over while writing. This keeps the tone of the script consistent throughout the length of the film and provides inspiration to the writer. This warm up is a great way for kids to make the connection between music and their storytelling. It's also a great way to get them unstuck when they're suffering from writers' block.

Heads Up #1: Don't use overly familiar pieces of score or this warm up will not work. If you play the march from *Raider's of the Lost Ark* by John Williams, the kids will only ever see Indiana Jones.

Heads Up #2: Always stipulate that the scene and the characters must be original. No scenes about Shrek and Donkey or scenes that take place inside the world of Mine Craft.

Bonus: Depending on the music you give the students, they will start expanding their writing to include scenes that take place in the future, in outer space, in a vast and empty desert or with characters that are not human. You'll get some really great responses from this warm up!

Need Some Music Examples?
"Knock the Cover Off the Ball" from *The Natural* by Randy Newman (heroic)
 "Alan Turing's Legacy" from *The Imitation Game* by Alexandre Desplat (heroic)
"End Credits" from *Field of Dreams* by James Newman (heroic and sad)
"End Credits" from *Serenity* by David Newman (action)
"Stargate Overture" from *Stargate* by David Arnold (adventure)

"Mural" from *Pleasantville* by Randy Newman (triumphant)
"Theme" from *The Day the Earth Stood Still* by Bernard Herrmann (old school sci-fi)
"Underwater" from *Big Fish* by Danny Elfman (mysterious)
"Underdog Saves the Day" from *Underdog* by Randy Edelman (cartoon heroic)
"The Pen is Blue" from *Liar, Liar* by John Debney (comical)
"Cavendish in Distress" from *Cloud Atlas* by Tom Tykwer, Johnny Klimek, and Reinhold Heil (comical and awkward)
"About Time Theme" from *About Time* by Nick Laird-Clowes (romantic)
"Punch Drunk Melody" from *Punch-Drunk Love* by Jon Brion (sweet waltz)
"Great Wisdom" from *Mr. Magorium's Wonder Emporium* by Alexandre Desplat (sweet)
"Bad Witch" from *Oz the Great and Powerful* by Danny Elfman (magical and dark)
"Snowdrop" from *Stardust* by Ilan Eshkeri (magical and mysterious)
"End Credits" from *I, Robot* by Marco Beltrami (dark & futuristic)
"Stingray" from *The Blue Planet* by George Fenton (lonely and dark)

Warm Up #4: Write a Scene that Integrates the following Sound Effect:
Play the students a sound effect. It could be waves crashing on a beach, a mechanical noise, a pig grunting, just about anything!
Listen to the sound effect and write a scene that uses it in proper screenplay formatting. Remember: a scene is a unit of action taking place in one location. A movie is made up of many scenes that move the story along, so your scene should be just one moment of a bigger story.

When they read their scene, play the sound effect when it is mentioned in the script!

<u>*Why this warm up*</u>? It is a great quick warm up for a day when you don't have much time and the kids get a kick out of hearing the sound effect when they read the script. It also reinforces proper screenplay formatting and we can never get enough practice with that.

<u>Heads Up</u>: As for the previous warm up, remind the students that the scene must be original.

Warm Up #5: Analyze a Short Film:
Find a short film (under 7 minutes) online. This could be one of the Pixar shorts, a short film by a college student, a film you've discovered at a film festival, or even a commercial:
Watch the short film and tell me who the protagonist is and who the antagonist is. Then map out these three elements of the plot: Catalyst, All is Lost, and One Last Shot.

Why this warm up? No matter how advanced your students are as screenwriters, it is hugely important to show them examples of short films. Pulling apart a short film or a commercial for story structure is quick and fun for the kids. If it is the first week of school, simply identifying the protagonist and antagonist might be enough. If it is later on in your program, identifying the "All is Lost Moment" will be even more helpful as they're trying to develop their own stories. Once you teach them the four types of endings, it can be fun to ask them to re-write the story with the three other types of endings. (See the screenwriting chapter for details.)

Heads Up: Even for these short films, negative comments should not be allowed in the conversation. Allowing smugness and criticism into your classroom is like opening Pandora's Box; you'll never get the kids back into thinking critically about positive aspects of a film.

Need Some Short Film Examples?
Pixar: *Luxo Jr., For the Birds, Lifted, Knick Knack, La Luna, The Blue Umbrella, Piper, Sanjay's Super Team, Presto*
Disney: *The Paperman, The Feast*
Borrowed Time by Andrew Coats and Lou Hamou-Lhadj
Mr. Hublot by Alexandre Espigares and Laurent Witz
Bear Story by Gabriel Osorio
Optomist by John Mervin
Bottle by Kirsten Lepore
Alma by Rodrigo Blaas
Junk by Kirk Hendry
Arctic Circle by Kevin Parry
Wire Cutters by Jack Anderson
Lost and Found by Caleb Slain
The Boy Who Loved the Moon by Rino Alaimo
The Cat Came Back by Cordell Barker
The Big Snit by Richard Condie
Stanley Pickle by Victoria Mather
Zero by Christopher Kezelos

Escargore by Oliver Hilbert
Star Crossed by Katie Aldworth
3X3 by Nuno Rocha
The Technician by Simon Olivier Fecteau
For the Sake of Health and Well Being by Justin Kroma
L.U.C.K. by Adam and Daniel Cooper
Contrails by Andy Richards and James Niebuhr
Thai Life Insurance Commercials: *Time, Street Concert, Silence of Love, Unsung Heroes*
True Move Commercial: *Giving*
     -Short Documentaries-
Ben Proudfoot: *Ink & Paper, Flying High, The Ox, Why This Road*
Smoke that Travels by Kayla Briët
A Supporting Role by Alex Bohs, Joel McCarthy, and Caleb Slain

Warm Up #6: Complete Four Types of Endings:
Create a setup for a short story that includes a character's wants and their needs. For example: *Meredith wants to go to see a scary movie with her friends but her mom told her she has to take her little sister along and she knows her little sister will have nightmares if she sees the movie.*

As a class figure out the Wants vs. Needs:
Meredith Wants: *to go see the scary movie with her friends*
Meredith Needs: *to be a positive role model for her little sister*

Four types of endings: Positive, Positive Irony, Negative Irony, and Negative

Possible Answers:
Positive Ending (gets what she wants AND what she needs):
Meredith is honest with her friends and convinces them to all go see the scary movie another time. They take her little sister to see a Pixar film.

Positive Irony: (doesn't get what she wants but gets what she needs):
Meredith feels conflicted by the peer pressure from her friends and finally decides to blow off her friends and takes her little sister to the Pixar film.

Negative Irony: (gets what she wants but NOT what she needs):
Meredith and her friends smuggle her little sister into the scary movie telling her they're going to see the Pixar film then feels horrible when her sister is traumatized by the scary movie.

Negative: (doesn't get what she wants OR needs):
Meredith and her friends smuggle her little sister into the scary movie but gets caught by the usher halfway through the film and gets kicked out of the theatre. By that time her little sister is already traumatized.

<u>Heads Up</u>: Obviously this warm up should only be given after you've had a chance to discuss screenwriting. (See the screenwriting chapter for details.)

<u>Why this warm up?</u> Young screenwriters often lament: "I just don't know how my movie should end." The seemingly endless possibilities for the direction of the plot can be overwhelming. Forcing them to come up with these four types of endings helps them get them un-stuck and makes their writing a whole lot more interesting.

Remember that warm ups should be fun and take no more than ten minutes at the beginning of class. Many of my students will look back at their warm ups for inspiration when they are planning an upcoming film project.

Part III: Behind the Scenes

My favorite insights into filmmaking are the director's commentaries on DVDs. It's fun to hear about production mistakes or about the meticulous way a scene evolved in the editing process. If I could go back ten years ago and have help of any kind, I would have wanted to view a student film and then have a DVD commentary discussing how that film was made including the pitfalls and lessons learned.   This is my version of a director's commentary. It's my way of pulling back the curtain so people can see how these films came together. These films can be viewed on our Vimeo channel.[13] I've chosen to discuss the films that were a "first" for our program since I've learned the most as a teacher from making them. I hope this helps as you are starting projects of your own!

---

[13] Cinematic Arts Academy Vimeo channel: https://vimeo.com/user8838627

Followed[14] (2007)
First Summer Film Project

Grade Level: 6
Ability Level: 2 years using iMovie and Final Cut Pro for school projects
Equipment: Tripod, Sony Mini-DV Camera, Boom Mic, Final Cut Pro 7
Length of Production: Pre-production: 4 weeks, Production: 2 weeks, Post-Production: 4 weeks

Before I ever had my own film class at Millikan, I had a film student. Cameron was in my 6th Grade English and history classes and I recognized right away that he was going to be a filmmaker when he grew up. There was just something about him. During that year I started to include options on our class projects to make a film. Cameron loved it and as the year wore on, I challenged him even further by asking him to create specific types of films. (*Example: Create a black and white Buster Keaton style silent film explaining the story of Odysseus and the Cyclops.*)

Cameron was not a typical middle schooler. For his birthday he got a copy of Final Cut Pro 7 and learned it well enough over Spring Break to be able to shoot and edit a film where one actor played multiple parts editing the performances together using the cropping tool. His dad, Jim, is a film composer and his mom, Karen, is a producer and neither of them had any background in editing. He learned the editing software himself.

At the end of his 6th grade year I had the opportunity at the school fair to sit down and talk to Cameron's mom about his summer plans.

"I'm so impressed with Cameron's work this year! Is he going to be able to continue making movies this summer?"

"We've looked into summer programs and there isn't much out there. The programs for his ability level don't take 12-year-olds and the programs for 12-year-olds are only teaching the basics of iMovie and Power Point."

"That's unbelievable!" (pause) "Well, I'll give him a reason to make a movie!"

Famous last words, Bennett. That began the summer movie projects that became a really wonderful and exhausting tradition for us.

---

[14] *Followed:* https://vimeo.com/230129334

Step 1: Pre-Production Pitch Meeting:
The first week of summer break I sat down with Cameron and his parents to talk about the project. I assumed he was going to do an adaptation of a short story but instead he came to the "pitch meeting" with a few story ideas that he was interested in pursuing. I swear the kid had an easel with story ideas on it and a ruler he used to point to the page during the presentation. The idea he was really excited about was a scary movie about a kid whose dad dies of a heart attack. The boy is then stalked by the Devil who wants to trade the boy's soul for the return of his father. Cameron wanted to challenge himself to make a scary movie but at that point the only scary movies he had ever seen were *The Ring* and the Nicholas Cage movie *Ghost Rider*.

Step 2: Screenwriting: I gave Cameron about a week to get me the first draft of his screenplay for the film. We decided the screenplay should be 5-10 pages. He wrote it in a Microsoft word document and emailed it to me for notes that I put in red and then emailed back. Because he had almost no experience with scary movies, parts of his screenplay were fairly awkward. Looking back, it would have been an excellent opportunity for me to discuss the psychological effect of camera angles and lighting to build tension, but it was my first time coaching a kid through the filmmaking process, so I'm going to cut myself a little slack. With a finished screenplay, we moved forward.

Step 3: Production: Cameron has always been a hard worker and very resourceful. He and his dad snuck his video camera onto a golf course to shoot the opening and closing scenes. His dad was a good sport and played the father in the film. Cameron played the son, setting up each shot and then walking to his mark. He worked out a schedule using his friends as actors and was able to shoot most of the scenes near and around his house.

The screenplay called for a few scenes at a middle school so I told Cameron he would have to present the project to our assistant principal in charge of summer school and ask permission for his film crew to be on campus. I knew it would be no problem at all and in reality I could have put in a call and it would have been a done deal in thirty seconds, but the point of a kid making a movie is to learn the movie making process and that includes securing permission for locations. Cameron came to school with a binder including sections for the screenplay, cast and crew information, and a shooting schedule. He sat down in front of our slightly intimidating assistant principal who listened politely, asked a few questions, and then granted permission.
When you shoot a scene at a school the biggest problem is securing extras. You need extras to be in the background consistently through each take and

kids at this age are just not good at that. They want to photo bomb your shoot or they lose interest and walk away causing continuity problems. I went to my friend who was teaching summer school choir and luckily he jumped on board to have his class be our extras for the film.

Step 4: Securing that Amazing Location: Cameron had a scene in his script that required him to shoot in a cemetery. He and his mom called all of the local cemeteries and were told they would not allow filming in their cemetery or they would allow it but at a huge cost and we would have to provide proof of insurance and security personnel. We decided to throw caution to the wind and just show up in the early evening at an out of the way cemetery. Here's the thing: kids at this age can get away with SO much because they're short and adorable. In years since I've had kids shoot scenes inside Target stores, gas stations, and even inside the LA County Museum of Art. You just can't do that when you are old and have lost the "cute" that goes with being a kid!

We arrived at the cemetery around 6pm (sunset was around 8pm), and the guy at the guard gate took one look at the adorable child who was making a movie for school and opened the gates. If we had called and asked, he definitely would have said no.

Caution: every year in Los Angeles I read about a student film crew that gets into huge trouble with the "ask forgiveness not permission" style of filmmaking. On November 29, 2015 students filming a school project were actually arrested when they caused a panic as people saw them walking near the 101 Freeway with what looked like real guns while shooting an action movie. Teach the kids to use good judgment, people.

Step 5: Onion Juice: After shooting the cemetery scene, Cameron needed to shoot the big night sequence where the boy confronts the Devil and turns down his offer to bring his father back in exchange for his soul. The Covells brought some work lights into their backyard and Cameron's brother, Chris, jumped in to help as cameraman. Unfortunately it was a huge, emotional scene for the main character and Cameron just couldn't muster up the tears to make it seem real. Jokingly I asked if anyone had an onion. Cameron bolted into the house, came out with an onion and knife, chopped it up, and rubbed it under his eyes. Not sure it worked the way he had hoped.

Step 6: Editing…Editing…D'oh! I got lucky with Cameron on this one. He loves editing and finished the rough cut of the film himself. I sat down a few weeks after we wrapped production with his family and we did a screening and notes session. Most of Cameron's footage in the cemetery had come back completely under exposed. He had lost the light and the camera couldn't handle it. The footage went from a little too dark but still manageable over time to being completely black. After he panicked and freaked out, he sat down at the computer, bumped up the brightness settings and finally came away with a super grainy black and white image. I wasn't familiar with his camera and should have known this would be a problem. Some things you have to learn the hard way.

Silver Lining: I think the sequence looks better in black and white with tons of grain. It's creepier and looks like an old 50's B horror movie in my opinion.

Step 7: Music: This is where I am most comfortable as a teacher because of my background as a music editor. I had a ball one afternoon teaching Cameron how to choose and edit music for each scene. We used *The Sixth Sense, Dead Again,* and *Dracula* soundtracks for the score. For anyone reading who doesn't have experience with finding music for a film here are a few tips:

1. Figure out the tone of your film and search online for other films that have a similar tone. *Followed* was supposed to be mysterious and dark with the Devil as a character. We listened to scores from the films that inspired Cameron to write the screenplay, *Ghost Rider* and *The Ring*, but both of them were off. *Ghost Rider* was way too action oriented and *The Ring* was way too dark. We expanded our search to other movies in similar genres and found our way to *The Sixth Sense*, which Cameron loved.

2. Try not to choose music from a film that is too well known. If you are placing music in an action scene and use the score from *Raider's of the Lost Ark,* the audience is only going to be able to think of Indiana Jones and it will distract from your film. I think our choice of *The Sixth Sense* was not optimal because the score by James Newton Howard was so popular at the time, but it was Cameron's decision and the score does work well in spite of it.

Since we were not going to put the film into festivals, we left the final film with James Newton Howard's music in it. This usage falls directly under the fair use act for educators.

Step 8: Premiere! We held a small premiere for the film at the end of the summer at the Covell's house. It was so important to have a celebration to wrap up all of the really hard work that went in to making the film.

Lesson Learned: I think the subject matter was too serious and too dark to make a good first film project. The things that scare us live mostly in our imaginations and in the shadows where we can't see them. Because of this, scary movies are the hardest films for young filmmakers to pull off successfully. It's a little like when you wake from a nightmare, heart pounding and head racing, your mind filled with the horrors that you just experienced and then you try to explain it to a friend. The things that were truly terrifying slip from your grasp in the explanation and no matter how hard you try to convince your friend that it was an experience straight from the world of Stephen King; it no longer is.

I would hold off on having young filmmakers try to tell a scary story until they have had time to study the screenwriting, production, and editing techniques specific to that genre.

Thriller[15] (2008)
First Whole Class Film Project

Class Size: 40
Grade Level: 7/8
Ability Level: No Experience, General Elective Class
School Equipment Available: Tripod, Projector, CD player (for music playback on set)
Personal Equipment Used: Canon ZR-850 Mini DV Camcorder, MacBook Pro, iMovie '08, Makeup for Zombies and Werewolf
Length of Production: Two semesters

The administrator who signed off on our summer shoot for *Followed* was nice enough to open one elective class for me to teach film that fall. I was excited and totally unprepared for planning a filmmaking curriculum for 40 students with almost no resources. I imagined having a classroom full of eager kids who couldn't wait to make a movie. I was wrong. The class had overflow from our other film teacher as well as a number of kids who didn't pick an elective and were simply assigned to my class. In other words, most of my students were the least motivated kids at the school. I remember the first day of class: my high-energy excitement for filmmaking was met with eye rolls and sighs. I knew I would need a film project that would be high interest, but not require too much difficulty. Something that was creative and offered lots of opportunities for fun work, but would not require an in-depth knowledge of filmmaking techniques. I needed to hook these kids and get them to like what we were doing before I even attempted to have them do anything too tedious, boring, or difficult (three words that aptly describe the vast majority of work in filmmaking).

Coming from a career in post-production I knew we were going to have a ton of trouble recording clean audio for a film on the ZR-850 since I only had the in-camera mic for sound. I didn't have a good handle on getting the kids to write a successful script at that point, so I went the easy route: music video. A few weeks into the school year on a whim, I showed the kids Michael Jackson's *Thriller*. With the exception of two kids, they had never seen it and they were blown away. Some of them downloaded the video on their phones and told me they watched it over and over that night. When I suggested we do a remake they were really excited and jumped on board. We would place our video over the original music video's audio track thereby circumventing the problem of having to record audio.

---

[15] *Thriller:* https://vimeo.com/232161775

Problem 1: Makeup Effects: I knew I'd need a ton of zombies for the remake, which would require my students to learn how to do zombie makeup. What a cool challenge in middle school!

I went on YouTube and found a few good tutorials and created a kind of illustrated chart showing the kids where to apply zombie makeup to a face. I bought a ton of grey, green, black, and yellow grease paint, sponges, and baby wipes from a local makeup store and practiced on myself until I thought I could pull it off.

Since I couldn't afford mirrors for all of my 40 students, we spent a week in class with the students applying makeup to their seat partners. It was actually my favorite time on the production since the students had absolutely no idea how ridiculous they looked and they ALL wanted to keep the makeup on when they went to their next class. This started some great buzz around the school about the project and brought the class together as a kind of family.

By the end of the week, we had three kids who were fairly proficient and could pull off a legitimate zombie face in roughly 10-15 minutes.

Problem 2: Can Anyone Dance? The answer was…no. More likely, "Hell no, I'm not dancing in a movie where the entire school will see it and potentially laugh at me," but the kids were polite and when I asked the class if anyone was interested in auditioning for Michael Jackson's lead role I simply got dead silence.

Movie making is all about having a Plan B, Plan C, Plan D, and an I'm-going-to-make-this-work-if-it-kills-me plan so I put out an announcement to the dance department looking for anyone, guy or girl, who was interested in being Michael Jackson. I literally got ONE volunteer. A shy kid I had never met who had trouble looking me in the eye. Sold! We have a winner!

I couldn't take the dancer out of class to film on all of the required days, so I sliced up the movie to have multiple Michael Jacksons: One for the werewolf in the scary movie bit. One for the walking past the graveyard bit. One for just the dance sequence.

Now we just needed the Werewolf MJ and the Graveyard MJ. No volunteers. I reminded all of the students that if the movie looked bad, we didn't have to put it in the film festival at the end of the year. No volunteers. I then promised we would take a vote when it was finished, and if even one person didn't want it screened, then we would not put it online or in the end of year festival. That got me my two remaining Michael Jacksons! Score!

Problem 3: Shoot and Scoot: Our class was 50 minutes each day, except on Tuesdays when we got 40 minutes due to early release for staff meetings. This means the kids would get to the classroom, put down their stuff, we'd take attendance, get the equipment out, wardrobe/makeup on, props accounted for, head out to the location, block, shoot, and get back before the bell rang. You don't need to be a filmmaker to understand what an insane way that is to make a movie.

We created a shot list based on the original film (an easy way to teach camera angles, so…bonus!) I turned the shot list into a storyboard for quick reference and cleared our locations with the staff at the school. In later years I would be able to have the students create the shot list, storyboard, and write letters to clear locations, but at this point I was still struggling with class participation and figured the quicker I could get to production (the "fun" part) the better.

Problem 4: 12-Year-Olds Love Zoom: There is something inherently spastic about the 12-year-old human being. They can't just let something be still. With every setup, I would walk the filmmaker through lining up the shot and then inevitably when they called "Action," they would put their hands on the camera and zoom or pan or tilt during the take. Why? They needed to feel like they were *doing* something! Each take looked jerky and spastic but I held my tongue because this was *their* learning experience. In hindsight, I probably should have intervened more…

Problem 5: Continuity? The werewolf scene included a girl being asked out by a boy who then transforms into a werewolf and chases her around the back of the school, trapping her at a locked gate and closing in on her. It took us three days to shoot. How do I remember exactly how many days? Because the lead actress has three different hairstyles and three different sets of earrings in that scene in the final edit. Did I talk to her about wardrobe and continuity? Yep. Did she listen? No. Have you taught middle schoolers before? They never listen the first time and I was so busy with everything else that I didn't take a picture for continuity and didn't notice.

The great thing is that in the years since making this film we've shown it to hundreds of people and gotten overwhelmingly positive reactions. Not once has anyone mentioned the three different changing hairstyles of our main actress in the werewolf scene.

Problem 6: The Nay Sayer: We edited together as a class, me on my computer and the kids watching via the projector and making decisions from their seats. Not ideal but it was all we had available. After editing a rough cut of the werewolf scene, I knew it was working. It wasn't Spielberg quality, but it was working! Excited, I asked another teacher if she'd like to see the first scene. She was a dear friend of mine and I figured she would be encouraging. Nope. She said three words to me after viewing the scene: "That's too bad." Then she threw her lunch in the garbage and walked out of my classroom.

The truth is that everyone, not just in Los Angeles, but EVERYONE is a critic.

Today, she's one of my biggest supporters and absolutely loves my successful program. If I asked her, I doubt very much that she would remember those three words.

Takeaway: Never show a friend your rough edit. It's seldom helpful. Even now when I'm having trouble with an edit, I've found that going for a walk and returning with a fresh perspective is far better than asking for someone's opinion. When my students ask me for an opinion on a rough cut I am always reminded of my friend's reaction and really think about the comments I give to the filmmaker.

Problem 7: No Dolly: You know that iconic shot where Michael has just left the movie theatre and is walking with the girl singing about how fun scary movies are? John Landis had a great dolly and someone to push the camera along to keep up with the actors. We had no dolly or grip equipment except for our tripod.

I put the song on a CD, found an old battery powered CD player, drew a map of the section of the school our Michael and the Girl would walk through and had the kids pan the camera to keep up with the actors who were lip syncing to the music. When they got out of range of the camera, we would cut, mark the location where they stopped with the lyrics on the map, move the camera, have the actors back up and take it from the previous line.

This was an insanely labor intensive way to shoot the scene. I should have put a kid in a wheel chair with the camera and wheeled them along with the actors and been done in 30 minutes.

It took us three days of after school shooting. Live and learn.

Problem 8: How Many Zombies Can We Get To Dance? The original music video has a ton of really cool zombies dancing with Michael Jackson. We had our one shy kid and no other volunteers. Digging around online I found the "Thrill the World" website. Some dancer in Canada wanted to teach the *Thriller* choreography to break the Guinness Book of World Record for biggest choreographed dance routine. I loved her teaching videos, bought copies, and enlisted the help of our dance department who had a free moment to spare at the very end of the school year after their final performances were over.

Unfortunately, the choreography videos were set to the radio edit of the song. In the music video, the zombie dancers only dance for 1:12 while the radio edit of *Thriller* is 5:13. I was so busy I figured we would just use the radio edit during the dance section of the film.

We shot the dance sequence on the hottest day of the school year. It was 103 degrees outside. My shy Michael Jackson dancer showed up with a real MJ style red leather jacket. Our location had no shade.

The dance students had been given permission slips to leave class early and queued up outside my classroom for their makeup. My film students created a Zombie Assembly Line, one kid doing the cheekbones then passing the zombie to the next kid for eye makeup, etc.

We got the dancers out to the location by 10am and did our first run through. My shy lead dancer and those directly around him absolutely *nailed* the choreography! Score one for the Millikan Dance Department! It was so hot the zombie makeup melted off after each take. The reapplication of the makeup got sloppier and sloppier as our film students were way more interested in watching the dancers than re-applying makeup. We got exactly three takes in the can and the dancers withered. That was it. If we didn't have the footage we needed, it was over.

Fun side note: I had lambasted all of the kids to wear sunscreen and then forgot to apply it myself. I got a serious, blistering sunburn.

Problem 9: No Time to Edit: Due to scheduling I couldn't control, the editing of the dance sequence wound up directly on my shoulders and had to be edited immediately so it could be premiered at the film festival the next day. I headed home with the footage, scratching my now oozing sunburn and edited straight through the night.

A note about iMovie'08: It's great if you're trying to edit together memories of your family vacation. It is absolutely uncool if you're trying to edit TO MUSIC. I'm lucky I was living alone because I'm fairly certain I swore loudly for ten straight hours trying to make the magnetic timeline in iMovie do what I wanted it to do. Why couldn't it work like ProTools? Why wouldn't it just let you stack takes on top of takes on the timeline so you can simply line up the dancers in time with the music? What the hell is this magnetic snapping tool that keeps jacking up my sync?!

Suffice it to say I have not used iMovie since that night. I forked over my personal money for Final Cut Pro 7 and later Adobe Premiere and found them both to be much more similar to my beloved ProTools and life has been much easier since then.

Crossing the Finish Line: I showed the class our entire finished movie the next day. They loved it and universally agreed to show it at the film festival. Due to the hype caused by the involvement of the dance department and so many students walking around wearing zombie makeup all year, it was highly anticipated. The line for the festival stretched far out the door. The audience loved it. Watching our kids lip-syncing with the original audio from the video made them laugh and cheer.

The absolute best moment was seeing one of my least involved tough kids arrive with his mom. She had hurried over after work still in her nurses scrubs looking exhausted. He took her by the hand into the auditorium. "We worked really hard on this movie, mom. You're going to love it!" I heard him rattle on about all the things we had done together to make the movie. I heard pride in his voice. I honestly didn't think he was paying attention through most of the process. I was exhausted so I went to the bathroom and cried.

Slenderman[16] (2012)
First Film with the Cinematic Arts Academy

Class Size: 35
Grade Level: 6
Ability Level: No Experience, Cinematic Arts Academy Class
Academy Equipment Available: None
Personal Equipment Used: Canon XF100 Camera, Tripod, MacBook Pro, Adobe Premiere & After Effects Editing Software
Length of Production: One Semester

Pulling Together the Brand New Cinematic Arts Academy: I taught general film elective classes for four years and when the previous film teacher took a job at a local high school, I stepped up and took over the film academy. The paperwork for the academy had been established a few years earlier, but it wasn't attracting students who could meet the school requirements of "no Ds, Fs, or Us on any semester report card to remain eligible for participation in an academy." The film academy students were dropping like flies. When kids would flunk out, the school would simply back fill the class with random students to maintain the proper class size and those students were not necessarily interested in filmmaking.

My first order of business when I took over the academy was to start recruiting from elementary schools in order to build a really solid incoming 6th grade academy class. I figured that if a student came to Millikan with the express interest of making movies, they might be more likely to maintain their grades to stay in the academy. Fall 2012 was my very first official academy class and I was so excited to work with these kids!

Step 1: Screenplay Trouble: As with my previous film classes, we started the year with basic camera angles and film terms. We discussed basic screenwriting and then the kids got to pitch a screenplay to the class. I always prided myself in taking whatever screenplay the students voted for and helping the kids to shape it into a workable film. I wanted them to have "buy in" for the project.

This particular year we had the *Slenderman* epidemic in social media. The kids were passing around stories about Slenderman during lunch and truly freaking themselves out so of course the screenplay my students voted to make was based on Slenderman. My student Michael had quickly become a leader in the class and wrote the screenplay based on a nightmare he had. The

---

[16] *Slenderman*: https://vimeo.com/92302599

screenplay was not school appropriate. I believe there was even a scene where a kid opens a locker and a severed head falls out with the eyes missing. It got an overwhelming majority of the votes. I couldn't allow my kids to make that film but I also didn't want to stifle their creative idea, especially after I had said that they would choose the movie we would make together. I kicked myself for not putting more emphasis on my policy of "no weapons, no violence" but the class had seemed so sweet and it didn't occur to me that they would come up with something so gory!

Step 2: Screenplay Problem Solving: The answer hit me: German Expressionism! If I could turn the character of Slenderman into a German Expressionist villain many of our problems would be solved. By definition, a villain in a German Expressionist film doesn't have a backstory or motive other than to be evil. I looked back at *Nosferatu* and *The Cabinet of Dr. Calligari*, two very creepy old movies that we could study the look of and dig a little deeper into film history while pulling from them to create our own scary (school appropriate) movie.

After reminding the class about our policy of "No Weapons, No Violence," we started to study German Expressionism and tweak our screenplay so it was about friendship overcoming great obstacles. We went "location scouting" on campus and took pictures of anything that reminded us of the lines and shadows that we loved in our German Expressionism research. The bars of a fence, the lines in a mural, the shadows of huge trees on a blank wall, our bright and colorful campus started to look a little creepy in black and white!

As we polished the screenplay, I played music in the classroom that might help set the tone for the film: Max Richter and John Cage were favorite composers since they were orchestral, but felt off kilter and "jacked up." I lovingly refer to our music choices in *Slenderman* as being the musical equivalent of food poisoning.

We quickly held acting auditions. Since all of the filming had to take place during our class period there was no way to get students outside the class to perform in our film. I get a lot of raised eyebrows from people outside the program when they see that our students are also the actors in the class films. We are, after all, a performing arts school with many wonderful student actors. I suppose I could check into drama classes at the same class period and hold auditions there, but something really wonderful happens when my filmmaking students are also the actors: they learn first-hand what actors need to be successful on set. It's a really excellent experience to be both in front of the camera on a film and then behind the camera on another film. It fosters humility and patience for the actor.

I explained which production jobs we would have for our silent film shoot: director, grip, lighting, and continuity. Each student wrote me a letter applying for one of the jobs. I created directing teams, one team for each scene in the movie, and we were ready to shoot.

Step 3: And...Action! We were using the Canon XF100 camera that I had purchased with my own money the previous year. The old ZR850s had died and I coughed up I think $3,000 for the camera thinking it was a good investment for the program. The XF100 is a camcorder in that it has a fixed lens with really reliable auto focus. The best part of this camera is that it has XLR inputs for a boom mic. Not that we needed audio on a black and white silent film but it was a smart investment. It worked great for these kids and we still use it to this day for documentary filmmaking. Our old school tripod that had been used on previous films died and I purchased a Manfrotto to take its place. Being a teacher can be really expensive.

Shooting *Slenderman* was an absolute joy. The kids in my academy were really well behaved and careful about blocking each scene and framing each shot. I remember mentioning we needed a small prop: a magnetic mirror for the inside of a locker. The following day I was kicking myself for not finding a mirror myself when three kids approached me with mirrors. This might seem like nothing, but in my experience with middle schoolers, they mean well, tell you they will do something, and then immediately forget. They are terribly unreliable. Stunned at their awesome contribution, we looked at all three mirrors and decided which one would work best for our shot. I wanted to hug every one of those kids!

While on set, if a student was not involved with a production team that day or working as one of the actors, they would storyboard each angle we were filming during the shoot. This kept them busy and reinforced their understanding of camera angles. It also allowed at the end of the period for "What if we?" shots. "What if we?" shots are something I came up with on Cameron Covell's set of *Dreamer* in 2008. Cameron was getting bogged down being overly occupied testing out interesting camera angles and running out of time to get basic coverage for each scene. He kept walking around his set of the 007 sequence saying, "Hey! What if we did a shot with his hands on his hips and the shot being framed through his arm? Hey! What if we put the camera super low to the ground like in *Citizen Kane*?" I finally put my foot down and said, "Cameron, you can get those *What if* we shots after you've gotten the basic coverage we talked about!" The term stuck and it became the way I deal with the effusive enthusiasm on set: get the basic coverage first, then go nuts with the time you have left playing with interesting and odd ideas that strike you at the last minute.

My academy kids love the idea of *What if we* shots. This was really the first class I ever had that could pay attention during shooting and give good feedback. They gave us great ideas for creative cut ins, cut aways, odd angles, and shots with interesting foreground elements or shots that reveal something in the scene through blocking. "What if we put the camera at a really low angle and showed only his hand reaching out for the ball with *Slenderman* in the background?" It was awesome.

Our wardrobe for *Slenderman* himself was a bit awkward. It was a plain white hood that zipped up the back of the head. We found it online and it worked great except that it did not afford our lead actor, Michael, to see anything. He enjoyed putting it on and pretending to walk into doors, walls, and garbage cans like the Three Stooges. Slenderman was getting less and less scary to the kids as we progressed in making our movie.

In the climax of our movie the protagonist is confronted by Slenderman and defeats him using the flash of a cell phone to trap him in a photo. We shot it out in our little farm area in the back of the school. As always, we had very little time to shoot and were going at an insane pace to get our shot list completed. At one point I turned, wondering why my students were being so noisy, and noticed my class had grown into a large crowd. Kids who were supposed to be working on the farm that period figured out what we were up to and wanted to come and watch. A little girl approached Michael (who was totally blind because he was wearing that stupid mask) and asked him for his autograph.

Step 4: Editing: We wrapped shooting and I put the footage on a designated hard drive. At this point I still didn't have any computers that the students could edit on so once again we were relegated to the kids watching on the projector and having discussions about how best to edit the footage. This broke my heart because I desperately wanted to teach editing and these kids were *so* eager to learn! The universe threw me a huge gift in a student who had already taught himself quite a lot in After Effects. I gave Tyler the footage on a flash drive and he took it home to do the VFX work for the shadow-on-the-wall shot. We also figured that we needed some way to enhance the goofy looking white Slenderman hood. It looked like a kid wearing a suit and a sock over his head. Luckily I had forced the kids to have almost all of the shots locked down on a tripod (to make the movie look more authentic to the filming style of the 1930s). Tyler and I simply cropped

Michael's head out of every shot of Slenderman and added a fast blur to it. Super simple. Totally worked. The rest of the class edited the film together throwing out suggestions as they watched via the projector.

Step 6: Premiere! We premiered *Slenderman* at our Winter Film Festival in January, 2013. It did really well with the audience and I felt confident that we could enter it in a few local student film festivals and possibly do well. Two of the students' moms closed in on me at the end of the festival promising to help me raise money for computers. I'm horrified to say that I rolled my eyes at them. If you're a public school teacher you know why I did: parents mean well and are constantly promising to help. Maybe one in one hundred ever follow through. Deana and Genevieve did follow through and it changed my entire outlook on teaching for the better.

A few days after the festival I was feeling kind of pumped up and excited about the prospects for my academy when one of my assistant principals walked into my classroom and confronted me about the film being *inappropriate*. He was very emotional and very upset. Was there a parent complaint? What was going on?

I had worked so hard to make sure that it was school appropriate. I had steered the kids away from severed heads in lockers and made sure that the message in the film was about perseverance and friendship. It had a positive ending. When I asked him to explain what specifically was inappropriate, he couldn't quite pinpoint anything specifically.

Finally he sputtered and said, "The music. The music was inappropriate and too scary."

I was shocked.

"It's instrumental classical music," I said, "What is inappropriate about classical music?"

He stammered and left my room.

In hindsight, truthfully we probably should have put a disclaimer on the front of the film at the festival because while Slenderman never touches or hurts anyone in the movie, it was creepy enough to give little kids nightmares. It honestly didn't occur to me that we would be able to make a truly effective scary movie. Never underestimate yourself or your students.

I submitted *Slenderman* to some student film festivals and it started to get really positive attention. It got into a film festival I had never heard of previously: The National Film Festival for Talented Youth in Seattle, Washington. We were invited to attend so I sent the screenwriter and actor, Michael, and VFX artist, Tyler, with their moms to go to the festival. They had an unbelievably positive experience with the older filmmakers at the festival one of whom said, "Wow! I thought German Expressionism was dead! Thank you for making that movie!" That experience lit a fire under my students at the festival. This movie lit a fire under our entire academy. The kids started working harder, paying more attention to the more subtle aspects of filmmaking, and they started to churn out better films.

Confronting #8[17] (2013)
First Film with Computers for Editing

Class Size: 38
Grade Level: 6
Ability Level: No Experience, Cinematic Arts Academy Class
Academy Equipment Available: Canon XF100 Camera (I donated it to the academy), Tripod (again, donated), Slider (homemade), 14 Computers, Adobe Premiere & After Effects CS6 Editing Software
Length of Production: One Semester

We Get Enough Money to Buy Some Computers: The summer after my first year with the academy, the parents pulled together and had a huge meeting to try to find ways to help buy computers for the class. They created a booster club 501(c)3 and helped me to rebrand my academy so we could attempt to find sponsorship. Millikan is a stones throw from Disney, Universal, and Warner Bros studios so it makes sense that they would want to support us, right? Not really. The calls we made to the studios went unreturned or were met with, "You're a middle school? Well, we only support college level or maybe high school level programs. Not middle school." It seemed to be the consensus that middle schoolers were too young to be supported as filmmakers. Oh, maybe they could toy around with stop motion Lego projects but there was no way they were going to make an actual movie.

Part of the rebranding was coming up with a new name for the program. The term "film" had always seemed so strange given that none of my students (and most of the pros) were no longer shooting on film. At our summer meeting with the parents we tossed out "Cinematic Arts" which lent itself to the word "camera" and decided on CAAM: Cinematic Arts Academy @ Millikan. We simply extended that for our 501(c)3 and called it CAAMERA: Cinematic Arts Academy @ Millikan Educational Resources Association. We purchased domain names and a parent helped me set up the websites for both CAAM and CAAMERA. Our CinematicArtsAcademy.com website has gone a long way to introducing people to our program. At this time I think we have more than 450 short films on the website along with information about the program, our festivals, and an online application.

We were able to cobble together some donated money and decided to spend it on seven iMac computers and seven MacBook Pro laptops. Using the educator's discount and purchasing older models, we were able to barely

---

[17] *Confronting #8:* https://vimeo.com/92270894

squeak by with these purchases. Our school had an old site license for Adobe Creative Suite 6 so we didn't have to pay for editing software and now we were in business! I was totally psyched! I had been itching to teach editing for six years!

Step 1: Another Silent Film: I have always maintained that the first film my students should attempt in the 6th grade should be a black and white silent film. It allows me to teach film history and emulate the simple, early filmmaking techniques with the class. Young filmmakers also tend to write too much dialogue. They will have their characters walk into a room and talk to themselves about everything they're about to do. I can't tell you how many student films I've seen with a kid sitting on a sofa watching TV who turns the TV off, sighs, and says to himself, "I'm so bored. I think I'll go outside and go skateboarding!" Nobody talks like that in real life. We just turn off the TV and go outside. Making a silent movie takes away the crutch of dialogue and forces the filmmaker to tell the story in the blocking, camera angles, and performances. Making a silent movie also lets me put off on teaching students how to capture sound on set until second semester. On a silent film set I can talk them through each take (much the way old silent movie directors would) and not have to worry about my voice in the audio.

The students pitched their screenplays and voted on a concept about a bully at a magic school. The screenwriter, Teddy, had all kinds of ideas about students riding broomsticks around campus. He didn't deny that he had drawn inspiration from the Harry Potter movies.

I brainstormed visual effects that would be fun, effective, and EASY: simple spark effects for the kids' wands, easy cropping for making objects appear and disappear in frame, and some practical effects too. Teddy and the class acquiesced to leaving out the flying broomstick chase scene and we polished the screenplay so that it would work in the silent film style. As with *Slenderman* when we began to polish the screenplay, I pulled music that seemed to fit the tone of the film to play at the beginning of class every day. It helped to keep the students focused and working towards the same tone for the film. For *Confronting #8* I pulled *Peter and the Wolf* by Prokofiev and *Academic Festival Overture* by Johannes Brahms. They are classical, slightly reminiscent of the 1930's for our silent film, and had themes that sounded academic and would also lend themselves to the bullying aspect of the script.

When making a movie about a bully at the middle school level, there's a conundrum: If you want to establish a character to be a bully, that character has to do something mean to another character. The question becomes: How mean is our bully? How much of a danger do they present to our protagonist? It can be a fine line to tread with your administrators and parents. Nobody likes to see bad or scary things happen in a school movie, but no movie will be successful without conflict. For *Confronting #8* we went with stuffing kids in garbage cans, and turning them into inanimate objects.

Step 2: Production: Using old choir robes from our music department made wardrobe super easy on this film. No hassle having kids run to the bathroom to change into wardrobe at the beginning of class! Each student had a felt number representing their magical strength pinned to their robe and the adults had robes from their own closets they brought in for themselves. We had several kids bring in Harry Potter wands they had from home, I used my old conducting baton, and our smallest actor (the comic relief) got a pathetic looking stick from outside and a Viking helmet to round out his costume.

Planning a shoot for Visual Effects turned out to be a bit more difficult to do with students than I thought. If it was just me behind the camera, I knew what would be needed for each VFX shot in post production. With kids behind the camera, I had to explain what the visual effect would be and what shots would be needed to composite together for the final VFX shot. Before our first day of shooting, for example, I needed to show an example of why we needed a clean plate so that the students on set would understand and not miss a necessary shot.

Speaking of clean plates: I am convinced middle schoolers have to mess up and bump the camera or tripod the first time they try to shoot a clean plate. No matter how much I explain and remind them, they *always* bump the camera or tripod and then try to convince themselves on set that it's "no big deal, I can just put the camera right back where it was in the first place so it will be fine." They think they've solved the issue until they try to edit the VFX shot in post-production and the clean plate has been slightly moved and can't be fixed. There will be tears. There will be anxiety. There will be reshoots. But they'll never bump the camera or tripod again while shooting a clean plate for a visual effects shot.

We shot over the course of three weeks and it started becoming obvious to me that I had bitten off more than I could chew with this project. I had planned for extra time in editing but I was getting the sneaking suspicion that I going to need more time in post if the kids were going to edit the film themselves. I had the kids come in on a weekend when the school was quiet to finish shooting and then I turned my attention to editing.

Step 3: Editing With Middle Schoolers: Editing in general is a fairly tedious process. For anyone who's never done it, it's a little like cross-stitching. You have lots of little things you have to do and you see the big picture develop very slowly. In fact, I've heard that's why in the early days of filmmaking they had women editors: the process of cutting and splicing film felt like sewing, which was considered women's work. It's really common for kids to get a rough assembly knocked together, take one look at it, get discouraged because it looks awful, and give up. The most crucial part of editing is in the tweaking you do after you finish the rough assembly.

To get a class of 38 middle schoolers to be proficient in editing you have to teach the basics of the editing software, then teach the art of editing: which shots go in which order and why. Finally you have to teach them how to polish an edit so you smooth out all of the awkward sections. I took the footage home and did a cursory edit of the first few scenes myself so I would know if (1) we really had all the coverage we needed and (2) if there were any problems that I'd need to help the kids work around. The footage seemed to be working in my estimation so I took the footage and the music and put it on their computers in the classroom.

I'd love to tell you that after six years waiting for this moment I effortlessly guided the class to creating a beautifully edited finished film; but that simply was not the case. I had mapped out each step of the editing process and how I would present it, but I had not fully anticipated the quagmire of 38 students interacting with our complex video editing software. I was overwhelmed with the kids' problems and questions as we moved at a sub-snail's pace through the first scene. I could tell them how to trim a clip and put it into their timeline, but with any middle school classroom, you tell the entire class something and only 40% really listen. Another 40% think they know already and only half listen, and the remaining 20% have their minds on what's for lunch. I made handouts with simple editing instructions, but kids at this age grew up with iPads and kid-friendly apps that you simply clicked around in until you understood how to play and that was the sum of it. Adobe Premiere is serious, professional video editing software! They were clicking around on every button and searching for the weird effects to play around with. Hands would pop up into the air when suddenly a kid would realize they hadn't been paying attention and had, in fact, totally fallen behind or screwed up something on their timeline.

Silver lining? If you ever want to really learn an editing program, put it in front of 38 middle schoolers and spend weeks walking around addressing every way that they've screwed something up:

"Ms. Bennett, I did what you told us to *(they didn't)* and it still doesn't work!"

"Ms. Bennett, my whole timeline disappeared!"

"Ms. Bennett, how come my screen is all zoomed in?"

"Ms. Bennett, my computer just died."

"Ms. Bennett, my clip is on the timeline but the screen is all black."

"Ms. Bennett, why is my footage all green?"

In the years since this first editing experience with the students, I've gotten really good at breaking down the editing process. Rule: If you think you've broken it down into easy to understand, bite sized pieces, break it down even further. Teach nothing but the interface and "what the buttons do" for two days. Teach titles for three days etc.

The kids got through the rough edit of *Confronting #8* by early December. We had fourteen rough edits (one on each computer) with no visual effects. I spent the next few weeks showing them basic cropping techniques in After Effects. We would spend half a class period watching me do the effect over the projector while they followed along with the handout I painstakingly created the night before, and then I would take them one step at a time through each visual effect. I would say half the class was frustrated and couldn't keep up. The next day I would do a re-cap for anyone who didn't have the shot "looking right" so they could start over and bring it up to speed then the entire class would continue at our snail's pace. At the end the kids figured out they had to pay attention all the time or they would fall behind. We also ended up with a few really good VFX shots from the kids. Luckily I didn't scare them away from After Effects for good and many of them went on to use the techniques I had taught them in their own homework projects.

I took all of their edits, pulling the best sections from each one into a master sequence, then smoothed it out and inserted their VFX shots. Many of the unfinished VFX shots I had to do on my own because we ran out of time before the Winter Film Festival. This was my fault because I did not anticipate just how much time we needed for editing. I could have dragged the project into the second semester, but I could tell the kids were burned out on the film (as was I) and we needed to turn our attention onto something new.

Step 4: Premiere: *Confronting #8* premiered at our Winter Film Festival. It was really well received by the audience. The score pieced together from *Peter and the Wolf* and *Academic Festival Overture* gave it the gravitas it needed. I was so exhausted from the experience that I vowed not to do anything that effects-heavy with the kids ever again. Famous last words, Bennett.

The Redemption of Allen Lineman[18] (2015)
First Off Campus Shoot with the Academy

Class Size: 35
Grade Level: 8
Ability Level: Advanced Cinematic Arts Academy Class (students with two years in the academy)
Academy Equipment Available: Canon 70D and Canon 60D, Tripod, Fig Rig, Jib, Softbox Lights, Rode Boom Mic, Adobe Premiere & After Effects Editing Software
Length of Production: One Semester

My very first class of Cinematic Arts Academy students would be graduating at the end of the school year and I felt like we needed a big culminating project to challenge them. I pitched the idea of an "off campus shoot" to our parent board the previous spring and they had really incredible ideas for locations. One of the parents was on the board of parks and recreation for Los Angeles and brought up the Paramount Ranch. I always told my students the one genre we would never be able to pull off was a Western given our limitations with shooting on our school campus and the enormous amount of work it would be to get the props and wardrobe together for a period piece. When I saw pictures of the Paramount Ranch my heart was set: we had to make a Western.

The Paramount Ranch is a piece of land up in Calabasas with an old Western town set that used to be owned by Paramount Studios back in the days when everyone loved Westerns and they were making them all the time. As enthusiasm for Westerns faded, the studio donated the land to the state and it became a public park. You can go there and walk your dog, hang out, and every now and then a production will rent the location for a film shoot. Los Angeles is actually a pretty cool city once you get beyond the tourist traps!

Step 1: Pre-Pre Production
Before I even let it slip to the students, the parents and I had to figure out if an off campus shoot was even feasible. Would LAUSD allow us to take kids there? Would we be able to shoot in the interiors of buildings? Where would the props and wardrobe come from? What about the sets?

Luckily, the Paramount Ranch is on the approved list of field trip locations for LAUSD. Our 501(c)3 afforded us extra insurance to permit shooting inside the buildings and just to be sure, Deana and Genevieve procured extra-

---

[18] *The Redemption of Allen Lineman:* https://vimeo.com/117706594

extra insurance to please everybody.

One of the parents had a relative working at the Autry Museum of Western Heritage and I spoke to her about a possible field trip with the kids to learn more about the Old West to help with their screenwriting. She did us one better: we would have a field trip with a free bus AND they would allow us to *check out* their extra items not being displayed by the museum to use for props and wardrobe! SCORE!!! A huge thank you to the Autry Museum!

Step 2: Pre-Production
The students were insanely excited about the prospect of shooting a Western. Filmmakers generally geek out over this challenge and we were no different. We watched Westerns, studied documentaries, researched the history of the Old West, analyzed the Sergio Leone "Spaghetti-Western" style of filmmaking, and listened to Ennio Morricone music at the start of class.

In early September we took a field trip to the Autry Museum. The tour guide was incredibly impressed by the kids' knowledge and enthusiasm. We walked around after the tour soaking in the details of life in the Old West: the carved mahogany bar, the display of sheriff's badges, the covered wagon; it all felt so relevant since we were about to make a movie about it!

We took another field trip a few weeks later to the Paramount Ranch. A docent dressed up like a rodeo cowboy took us on a tour, explained the history, then the students were given an assignment: Location Pictures. They were to find all of the nooks and crannies of the location and take pictures for us to refer to when writing the screenplay. They had a ball and when we got back to school they were ready to write.

We had phenomenal ideas pitched to the class but the script that won the vote was called "The Revenge of Allen Lineman." The screenwriter, Jeremy, envisioned a gun battle, lots of action, and some really fun one-liners. Because we have a "no weapons, no violence" policy for our academy, we had to really consider the presence of guns in our film. It would be disingenuous to leave them out because they were a huge part of the Western genre. On the other hand, I did not want to glorify gun violence with my middle schoolers. I wrote a letter to our administrators asking for permission to include guns in our film. I promised the gun props would never be handled by the student crew or used by any child actor in the film. I promised that gun violence would not be glorified and the consequences of using a gun would be realistically portrayed. My administrators trust me in my work with the students and gave me the go-ahead.

We polished the screenplay over the next week or so. For our class that means pulling apart the story and isolating the protagonist's journey: what is their goal? What is their character flaw that keeps them from their goal? We rolled this around the class and it started to become apparent that our protagonist is selfish and therefore needs *redemption*, not *revenge*. With this new motive in mind, we began to build out the backstory and knew we needed it to end with a showdown in the middle of the town (I mean, we couldn't pass up an opportunity to shoot a showdown!!!) This is a little bit of the tail wagging the dog, but in this situation we found it necessary. To show Allen Lineman being selfish, we determined he is a famous gun slinger that left a town full of outlaws to look for fame and fortune elsewhere and immediately after he did an outlaw came and killed the townspeople, robbing them and subsequently spreading a rumor that Allen Lineman had done it. With a bounty on his head for the murder of the townspeople of Reddington, Allen wanders aimlessly in his guilt until he comes across a small town looking for some water and bumps into his nemesis. We kept working the script until we had it sufficiently full of our favorite Western moments all while bringing the character of Allen Lineman into a position to redeem himself at the end in a showdown.

Step 3: Enlisting Extra Help and Casting: At this point I worried that once I got the students, equipment, props, and wardrobe to the Paramount Ranch, we might have trouble with the crews during filming. My students knew how to use the equipment but I thought they might be nervous on such a big set and not be efficient or if they had questions I might not be readily available to help as I bounced between multiple crews. Luckily I had two former students who were up for the task of crew wrangling and they were really excited to pitch in. Cameron Covell was now twenty years old and at USC and Alex Brisker was now a senior in high school at the Los Angeles County High School for the Arts and both were filmmakers. I sat them down for a pre-production meeting and they gave me their thoughts on the script, then I gave them our list of scenes and film crews each one would be responsible for chaperoning. Having these two former students to help keep the crews on schedule and help the kids troubleshoot any problems that came up was a huge relief!

In addition to Cameron and Alex, I also needed a few good actors. I was fairly certain that a professional actor would balk at the idea of shooting an eleven page Western in two days with multiple film crews all between the ages of thirteen and fourteen. I needed actors with a sense of humor, patience, and who would work well with kids. I immediately called Pete Gardner who I've known ever since his oldest son was in my first class at Millikan and whose younger son was currently in the program. Pete jumped on board, searching for his own wardrobe and even using effects makeup to create a nasty looking scar on his face to make the character of the evil Sheriff look like he had a violent past. Pete is a professional actor and I knew his presence on set would be really fun for my young directors.

For the character of Allen Lineman, I called up a former teacher and friend who left the profession to pursue acting. Bobby Gilliam is one of the best math teachers I've ever seen. He not only likes kids but he also has that air of authority that comes from being a teacher. I knew that if we were filming a scene and something goofy happened, he'd be an ally to me in ironing it out and getting everyone focused. On top of that, he *looked* like a guilty cowboy and has some mad acting chops. I pitched him the project and he loved the idea.

Now we needed two sheriff's deputies. I went straight to Matt Gardner (Pete's oldest son) who is an incredible actor and comedian. Matt is the kind of actor that is effortlessly funny. I have a ton of fond memories of him as a student in my English class; he's that kid that lights up a room because he's sweet, joyful, and oozes natural talent. When he accepted the part, we went back and tweaked his lines a little to make his character the slightly less intelligent comic relief.

The easiest call I made was to Skyler Millicano who is a former student of mine and currently works as a stunt actor at Universal Studios. Skyler and I go way back and he's worked on the vast majority of films I've ever done with kids. He calls me "Mom." Because I got Skyler on board, we were able to also utilize his talent as a fight choreographer. Bobby Gilliam might be the best math teacher I've ever seen, but Skyler is the best TEACHER I've ever seen. Period. He can teach anyone how to do complex fight choreography in no time flat and have them looking super slick no matter what their experience level. I'm constantly amazed at his abilities and couldn't wait to have him work with my students.

The last two lead parts to cast were Daniel and his mom, Charlotte. We held auditions in my classroom and it was immediately obvious that Michael clearly had the passion and the talent to handle the part. Bobby Gilliam was his math tutor; so their friendship was going to be an easy sell on screen. The role of Charlotte went to Elizabeth Lambert, a friend of one of the parents. The subsequent parts would go to students in our class and teachers from our school.

Step 4: Procuring Props and Wardrobe: Two of our students, Delana and Maya, were responsible for props and wardrobe. We met our parent volunteers, Deana and Genevieve, at the Autry Museum about a week before the shoot to dig through their extra inventory to dress our sets. The little back room was full of stuff: cups, toys, equipment, signs, fake food, animal skins, clothes, and baskets. We took everything we could, keeping a careful inventory of the items for the museum records. We loaded them into our cars and stored them in my classroom.

What we couldn't find at the Autry Museum, we farmed out to the parents and students. As items came in, we kept records. Deana's brother had a collection of replica Old West guns (not real but very realistic) and some furniture items came in as well. The hardest item to find was a table for the Saloon. It needed to be huge and wooden to match the time period but that was going to be insanely difficult to move even if we had one. Looking at the weird pile of Western stuff in my classroom I figured that we could use a folding card table and put a cowhide on top of it with four wooden chairs and that would be acceptable.

What we couldn't get donated by the class, we purchased online and at Goodwill using some of our fundraising money. We needed huge iron keys for the jail and a few pieces of wardrobe. I think we spent less than $200 altogether on props and wardrobe!

On Friday after school, Deana rented a U-Haul and we loaded up all of our props, furniture, wardrobe, and equipment. That night we were informed we were not permitted to dig into the ground at the Paramount Ranch. It was part of their contract and we couldn't break the rules. We needed a cross at a lonely grave and had no idea how to put a wooden cross in the ground without digging. One of the parents, Frank Endewardt, came to the rescue and constructed a cross with a simple base stand. I went home and inventoried then checked and re-checked all of the film equipment and answered last minute emails from parents and crewmembers.

Step 5: And...ACTION! The morning of the first day of the shoot we arrived at 6:30am and waited in the parking lot for the park ranger to check our paperwork and allow our U-Haul to drive into the Paramount Ranch. We had call sheets, crew lists, shot lists, our day was broken down meticulously and yet we all knew on any film set the best laid plans can fall to pieces in a moment, especially when your crew consists of middle schoolers.

When we were finally allowed on location, we set up our wardrobe and equipment in the sound stage (a modified barn with electricity) and everyone got to work. Deana and Genevieve took control of getting the interior locations in order, Cameron and Alex met with their first crews for the day, our actors got into wardrobe, and everyone went to their first locations. We were going to start shooting on the jail set first. We schlepped in some of the bags with animal pelts and opened one up. It was a bag of skunk pelts. No joke. The Autry Museum lent us a bag of skunk pelts and they smelled…fresh. Not wasting any time, we used the pelts to camouflage anything that looked "modern" and set up our lights, tripod, and camera. We did a quick run through for blocking and then we heard the noise...

You see anyone can be at the Paramount Ranch because it is a public park; if you want it to yourself, you have to pay a ton of money that we didn't have. We planned on a few people that might need to be steered around what we were doing, but we had NOT planned on a weekend full of professional photographers corralling large families, engaged couples, and seven women modeling wedding dresses on our set. One couple came by during a take and asked if they could get a picture with the cowboys. Another simply placed their adorable infant into our scene "just to get a quick picture." A photographer on the other side of the jailhouse wall can be heard in the audio shouting at a large extended family, "Okay, now everyone smile! Oh, where is little Jacob, he's wandering away, can anyone grab Jacob and get him back in the shot? Jacob?" *clap clap* "Jacob look at me, Jacob! Look at the funny man with the camera, Jacob!" We had to station a parent at every door to our sets because while we had paid the extra money for insurance to be allowed on the interior of the buildings, the tourists did not, and they were not taking "no" for an answer. We had lots of belligerent people insisting that they were allowed on our interior sets because "this park is open to everyone." We had a tour group on horseback go right down the middle of the set twice. I gave them the stink eye the second time they ruined a take and the group leader gave me the middle finger.

It was incredibly hot and the actors and crew were melting. The sound stage was relatively quiet and cool so that's where most people were when not defending our sets or shooting a scene. The kids miraculously were working quickly and not complaining. Frank Endewardt is a professional grip and parent of our student, Eda. He was there the entire time wrapping cable, moving locations, giving advice but not stepping on any toes. The kids became enamored of his ability to wrap and throw cables. I'm serious, that guy makes cable wrapping an art form! He was also our designated gun handler. He was the only one allowed to touch, move, or handle the fake guns on set when the actors weren't using them for a scene. We wanted to be very careful about sticking to industry standards about managing guns on set.

The morning crew left and the afternoon crew arrived. I went over to the Saloon and my jaw dropped looking at the beautiful set. The kids under the watchful eye of Deana and Genevieve pulled off a real Western saloon set!!! I just about cried but then a tourist came barging in and that was the end of the beautiful moment.

The end of the first day came at sundown around 5:00pm. We had to pack everything into the U-Haul. Nothing was secure, so we couldn't leave anything there overnight.

Checking Footage that Night…
Wanting to make sure we had all of the footage from the first day, I went home and immediately began transferring it onto my backup hard drive. I spot-checked and realized the scene in the jailhouse had NO audio for the second half of the morning. It appeared that someone hadn't plugged the boom mic into the camera all the way and the sound person hadn't caught the problem (even while wearing headphones?!?) No time to be upset, I called Cameron and Alex and let them know that we would be shuffling the shooting schedule to accommodate one take of the jailhouse scene in the morning before we began the rest of the shooting schedule. This way we would have *some* usable audio to work with in that scene in post.

I plugged all of the batteries in to charge, checked all of the cameras for problems, and cleaned the lenses. I re-checked the batteries in the boom mics, re-checked the XLR cables just to be sure they were still working. I scrubbed the dirt clods out of my ears and from under my fingernails, and went to bed. If we don't get enough usable footage, I told myself, we would take what we've got and make a Western music video or experimental film. So much of this is beyond my control.

Day Two…
The second day was easier in that we knew the challenges we would be facing and were prepared. I had a meeting with the crews and we plotted to keep people out of our way when we were filming posting lookouts to keep people from accidentally wandering into the shot. God bless our actors and Cameron and Alex. They kept their spirits up, had a sense of humor, and kept shooting at a break-neck pace. We had an eleven-page script and two shooting days and they made it happen.

There was one moment that stands out to me about that shoot. It was sometime in the second day of shooting when I was wrangling production and looked up to see the crew. My former students, Matt, Skyler, and Cameron were walking my current students through the shot. Cameron has his hand on Jeremy's shoulder as he's guiding him backwards with the camera and Matt has Michael in a headlock. Seeing my former students guiding my new students struck me as an unexpected milestone in my teaching career. Someone took a picture and it's my favorite thing in the world.

By the time we shot the showdown that evening, we had a designated place for tourists to come and watch. Most of them wished us well and complemented the kids on their hard work. There was a sense of satisfaction as we set up each of the iconic shots. I enjoyed watching Bobby and Pete getting ready to perform their "quick draw." They looked like they were channeling their childhood somehow. It's really something special to witness.

The sun went down, we packed the U-Haul and whether we had all the footage we needed or not, we were finished with production.

Step 6: Post Production
It took me a few days to look through the footage from multiple cameras and get everything sorted into folders labeled by scene. Our computers in the classroom didn't have enough hard drive space and we didn't have external hard drives for each computer, so I spent time sifting through the footage and trashing unusable takes.

The first order of business was to have the kids watch the footage from each scene and label the best takes. It should be mentioned here that it doesn't matter how advanced my middle school filmmakers are; they will ALWAYS spend time looking for the most awkward frame and make a still image out of it to enjoy later on. It's usually an up-the-nose shot or one frame from a dramatic scene that when viewed by itself looks hilariously spastic and awkward. I've learned to give them time to laugh and appreciate the goofy moment, then we move on.

I allowed the kids to start their edit with any scene in the film. Most of them wanted to begin with the showdown because…it's the *showdown!* After about a week into editing, I was walking around checking progress and noticed nobody was editing the scene inside the Saloon. It's a scene with a lot of dialogue and no action so of course it was less interesting than the others. I began to assign scenes to the editing groups. This was hugely disappointing to the kids at first, but they seemed to understand why I did it.

At this point my student Josh came to my desk and said that he had ideas about the score. He wanted to write some guitar music and record it with his dad playing percussion for the soundtrack. I had no idea how advanced he was as a musician but I knew it was a bigger task than he understood. It's one thing to come up with a cool guitar theme, it's another to figure out how to write music that would accompany a chase scene or underscore an ominous conversation. Instead of trying to explain the difficulties, I just told him to go for it. I figured he would come up with something usable or it would be too difficult of a task and he would give up. Either way it would be a great learning experience, so why not? While Josh was writing music, the rest of the class was using James Newton Howard's score to *Wyatt Earp* as temp music.

At some point in early December, we started getting finished scenes from the students. I did several mini-lessons on cleaning and fixing audio. The scene inside the jail we cobbled together using the audio from just one take. We didn't do any ADR and when we layered the ambience, sound effects, dialogue, and music; it started to look and sound like a real Western! There were a few small VFX shots that I threw to Tyler who had continued to go above and beyond in After Effects ever since we did *Slenderman*.

After winter break, Josh sent me his music. It was absolutely amazing! I think it sounds just like a Spaghetti-Western! The class had fallen in love with their temp score but Josh's music would be absolutely perfect over the end credits.

Step 7: Premiere: Approaching our Winter Film Festival, Bobby Gilliam was getting a little nervous about his performance and whether he could carry the movie as the lead actor. I invited him over to my house for a screening. We watched it together and when it was done he simply said, "Yep, that's good. I'm good with this. Thanks, I feel better." It's one thing when your performance is in the hands of a professional filmmaker, it's another when it's in the hands of multiple middle schoolers.

I also held a screening of the film for Deana and Genevieve in my classroom after school one day before the festival. The three of us had worked like mad to create the academy and this movie represented all we had hoped to do for the students. I can't say it enough: nobody makes a movie on their own. I was so fortunate to have a dedicated and talented group of parent volunteers.

Millikan Votes 2016[19] (2016)
First Documentary with Students

Class Size: 35
Grade Level: 6
Ability Level: 6th Grade Cinematic Arts Academy Class (students in the first year in the academy)
Academy Equipment Available: Canon XF100, GoPro, Tripod, Monopod, Rode Interview mic, Adobe Premiere & After Effects Editing Software
Length of Production: One Semester

I delayed teaching documentary filmmaking until my 5th year into the Cinematic Arts Academy. I love and respect documentary films and found working on my own documentary *Pink Slip*[20] and the BlueField Productions project *Go Public: A Day in the Life of an American School District*[21] to be very rewarding. My concern was that documentary filmmaking is less flashy than narrative films. Middle school students love being able to tell a funny or scary story of their own design and documentaries just feel dry in comparison. Documentaries in my estimation also require extraordinary patience and intelligence on the part of the filmmaker. In narrative filmmaking, you create a script then use that script as a roadmap when you shoot and edit your film. In documentary filmmaking the process is backwards. You come up with a topic and then shoot your interviews and B roll hoping that somewhere in that footage will be your story. To say the least I was worried about how a documentary project would be received by my 6th graders.

In the summer of 2016 I decided it was finally time to give documentary filmmaking a go with my students. Our topic would be about the upcoming school Mock Presidential Election. Our Civics Academy was in its last year and the students were going all out to create a school wide opportunity for every student on campus to cast their vote for the presidential candidate of their choice on the same day that the country would also be voting. I was very impressed by the organization and passion of the Civics Academy leadership. The civics students passed out folders with handouts explaining the process by which the presidential candidates are selected and how the voting process works including information about the Electoral College and a history of both the Democratic and Republican parties.

---

[19] *Millikan Votes 2016:* https://vimeo.com/199105115

[20] *Pink Slip:* https://vimeo.com/30295251

[21] Go Public Project: http://gopublicproject.org

In August as the students came back to school, I started to get an awful feeling that I was walking into quicksand with this project. I was watching the presidential debates from the perspective of a teacher that was about to have to explain the snarky and often-inappropriate comments made by the candidates. I had envisioned a documentary about policy positions and polite differences on social issues and that simply was not the way the country or the candidates were handling the campaign. I heard students on campus discussing the election and shouting angry words at students who supported the other candidate. Newspaper articles about students harassing Hispanic students with "Build a Wall" chants on campuses around the country started to get me nervous. Several mock elections at nearby schools were cancelled as teachers and staff anticipated students becoming aggressive or verbally abusive to each other on the day of the election.

I went to the teacher of the Civics Academy, Erin Tanguay, who steadfastly maintained that we would have the mock election and it would be a wonderful civic experience for the school. I asked her what she wanted her own students to understand about the election. She said she wanted the students to be empowered by the process so when they turned 18 they wouldn't be one of the huge number of young people who stayed home on election day. She was looking to increase civic engagement in our community. For her, it wasn't about either candidate, but about young people exercising their right to vote and make their voice heard. Now THAT I could sell in a documentary! Our conversation further clarified the goal of the project for me and I went back to my classroom with a sense of relief.

Step One: Pre-Production: Research, Research, Research: Getting students to "ask good questions" is a massive goal in education that permeates all subjects. What I needed for this documentary were students who could prepare smart, open ended questions to ask people they would interview, and then train my students to ask intelligent follow up questions on the fly without any help from me. To get the kids ready to ask good questions, they needed to know as much as possible about the election process and the policy positions of the two leading candidates. I spent three weeks in August doing nothing but having the students research. I brought in several kid friendly articles on the candidates and had them learn what the bigger policy issues were. Then we brainstormed a list of questions they could ask of teachers, students, and Mock Election leadership. I thought I might have to tweak their questions but truthfully, they did it all themselves:

Teachers:
       Why is the mock election important to your students?
       How do you hope the Mock Election will impact the students later in life?

What issues in this election are most important to your students?
As a history teacher, what would you like the next generation to know about voting?

Students (voters):
How did it feel when you finally cast your vote?
What is the most important change you'd like to see the president make?
What was your favorite part of the mock election?

Ms. Tanguay (Civics Academy Teacher) and Mr. Plevack (Principal):
Why is it important for students at this age to vote in a Mock Election?
How has this Mock Election been different from others at Millikan?
What is your favorite memory of the Mock Elections?

We wanted to make sure our interview subjects were given the opportunity to discuss the issues of the election but we needed to be careful and ask questions that would not lead to enflamed, partisan answers. We kept the questions about the voting process and issues, and deemphasized the horse race that the presidential election was becoming.

Step Two: What Makes a Good Interviewer? I had to find several students that could serve as our on-camera interviewers on the day of the mock election. We had many students interested in being the interviewer, so we did an "Interview Challenge" that served as an audition process. We were looking for confidence, eye contact, and good follow up questions. Each student would come up in front of the class following my simple guidelines and interview me using our interview questions.

Interview Guidelines:
1. State the question clearly and be able to explain it or break it down if the interview subject has any questions.
2. Politely remind the subject to use the question to begin their answer. (Example: Question: What is your name? Proper Response: My name is Joe Schmoe.)
3. If an answer is too long or unclear, politely ask for a restatement of the answer.
4. Ask follow up questions:
    a. This means that you are listening to the response and asking for further information based on what they say. (Think: Why is this important? How did this happen? etc.)
5. Never interrupt or "step on" the response of a subject:
    a. If a subject interrupts you to begin responding, immediately STOP speaking and let them answer the question! (We

don't want your words mixing with their words as you're speaking over each other!)
   b. Even if the subject is rambling, let them finish their thoughts before you ask for clarification or a restatement.
6. Always look your subject in the eyes and pay attention to what they are saying.
7. Never allow yourself to react or make a facial expression that shows that you disagree with the subject.
8. Stand tall and don't slouch!
9. Allow yourself to be still and hold the microphone still.
   a. No playing with your hair, bouncing, or fiddling with mic, your clothes, etc.

Step Three: Logistics: We kept the filming crews small: Interviewer, Camera, Grip, and Sound. Because our mock election was only one day and we would never be able to do reshoots if we had trouble, our principal agreed to allow me a sub for the school day. Each crew in turn would come to the lawn where the mock election was held and film for one class period each. We had a crew come in before school to film the set up and a crew after school to film the ballot counting. Another crew was scheduled to shoot the next day when the election results were announced to film student reactions.

B Roll: Each crew was responsible for some element of B-Roll during their shoot. The students made a list:
- ☐ Hands dropping ballots in the box
- ☐ Kids posing with the candidate cutouts
- ☐ Kids in groups modeling their "I Voted" stickers
- ☐ Flags and election decorations
- ☐ Lines of voters
- ☐ Voting Booths (not inside, but maybe from behind?)
- ☐ Kids getting their registration cards from Civics Academy students
- ☐ Bake Sale
- ☐ Ms. Tanguay giving help to students

Each interviewer got a card with the basic interview questions on it (a copy was kept with me in case they lost or dropped the card).

I contacted several history teachers with photo/video release forms so we would be able to ear mark some of their students for on-camera interviews.

Step Four: Action! Our mock election was surprisingly subdued! The rest of the country was in a frenzy on election day, but the students at Millikan were patiently waiting in line for their ballots and voting.

It turned out to be an incredibly hot day, so our idea that we would spontaneously interview people as we walked around the event was not going to happen. We set up our interview crew behind the ballot box under a tent. Our earmarked students found us and did a beautiful job talking about the election on camera. The crews even got more B-Roll than I thought we would.

I have made a ton of movies with students over the years. Every movie has challenges. For all of the challenges I envisioned for this documentary, it turned out to be one of the easiest projects I've ever done as a film teacher.

After school, our students filmed some B-Roll as Civics Academy Leadership students counted the ballots. We went home and watched the results come in from the real election.

As it turned out, Hillary Clinton won our mock election while Donald Trump won the real election. The crew that filmed the reactions of the students the next morning had a rough time. When the winner of the mock election was announced, we figured we would have a big response. We did not. The class we filmed was overwhelmingly not happy with the results of the real election and our opposite result seemed to rub salt in the wound. Several of the students agreed to be interviewed and spoke beautifully about their feelings.

Step Five: Editing: I put the footage on the students' computers and walked them through our workflow. I gave them a few days to sift through the footage and tag clips that were interesting, well spoken, or amusing. I asked them to start with the interview of the teacher, Ms. Tanguay, who could give a good framework explaining what the mock election is all about. Then the students went to the interview footage and found sections that gave the best responses. Finally, they went to the B-Roll to add connective elements between the interviews.

Over winter break, I took their project files and opened up their timelines on my own computer and simply copied and pasted the best sections of the project files into a final timeline. I left spaces where we needed montages of B-Roll footage and put the final project file onto all of the classroom computers for the kids to finalize when we came back from break. I taught them how to create lower thirds to identify the interview subjects and we searched for music on royalty free music websites.

Step Six: Premiere: We premiered *Millikan Votes 2016* at our Winter Film Festival just a few days after the inauguration of Donald Trump. We are a school in Los Angeles, so it is not going to surprise anyone that our audience was generally not happy with the new President of the United States. I worried that the audience would have political burn out by that time of year and not want to spend time thinking back on Election Day. I was wrong. The theme that I had discussed with Erin Tanguay way back in August shone through: our audience was encouraged by the enthusiasm of the young voters and our documentary filmmakers. I had several comments that the documentary made people feel better knowing the next generation was educating themselves about politics and would likely be involved in the voting process when they turned 18. Hopefully that is true and when these 12-year-olds turn 18 they'll remember this experience and head to the voting booth.

Final Thoughts

As my students progress through my three-year program, there is less need of these huge class film projects. Our last class film, *Still,* had student crews that were so advanced they no longer needed that step by step group filmmaking experience. There was a bit of "too many cooks spoil the broth" on set as their ideas clashed with one another. One crew wanted to light a set a particular way and another crew had other great lighting ideas creating continuity issues in the lighting between scenes. I began to feel like our group project was holding them back a little bit. I have several ideas that I'll be implementing in the next few years to challenge these extraordinary advanced young filmmakers and we'll see how it goes.

For inexperienced students, however, creating these class films continues to be an invaluable tool for teaching students each step of the filmmaking process. It gives them the opportunity to step into each role on set and be a part of the filmmaking process from start to finish. It lets them know what work on a film set is supposed to look like so they can go off on their own and be successful in their own filmmaking.

If you begin to pursue filmmaking with middle schoolers, cut yourself a lot of slack and take it slowly. I love to remind myself that nobody makes a movie alone. The truth is nobody teaches students how to make a movie without a massive amount of help.

I hope you find a student like Cameron to start your journey. He taught me to have a sense humor on set and to never underestimate a talented kid with a weird idea.

I hope you find friends like Jim and Karen Covell and Alison Farr who taught me that it's okay to step forward and lead a kid through the filmmaking process even if you aren't completely sure you're capable of doing it.

I hope you find friends like Genevieve Colvin and Deana Payne who started the Cinematic Arts Academy with me. They taught me that parents of students every now and then offer the world to a classroom teacher and then deliver.

I didn't do any of this alone. Thank you to my family, friends, colleagues, and above all: my students.

ABOUT THE AUTHOR

After receiving a degree in Film Scoring from the Berklee College of Music, Karen Bennett worked for four years as a freelance music editor on such films as *Tim Burton's Planet of the Apes, Star Wars: Episode II: Attack of the Clones, Harry Potter and the Prisoner of Azkaban,* and *Catch Me If You Can*. In 2004, she transitioned into teaching. It was an easy decision; Karen loves working with kids and finds inspiration in their view of the world.

In 2007 she began teaching a film elective for students curious about filmmaking and created the Cinematic Arts Academy in 2012. Also in 2012 with the help of a grant from Funds for Teachers, she spent four weeks in Tanzania learning about the history of the country and visiting schools, documenting the trip with her video camera. In 2015 she won the *Crystal Apple Award* for innovation in teaching from the Los Angeles County Office of Education.

When not working with her students, Karen enjoys making independent films of her own. In September 2011, Karen finished her first feature length documentary, *Pink Slip*. In May 2012, she was hired as one of fifty directors shooting the documentary *Go Public: A Day in the Life of an American School District* produced by Jim and Dawn O'Keeffe.

Today Karen continues teaching at Millikan and traveling to film festivals around the world with her students including the Giffoni Film Festival in Italy, the National Film Festival for Talented Youth in Seattle, Washington, and the All-American High School Film Festival in New York City.

Made in the USA
Middletown, DE
01 April 2023